D1479201

Prisons under the Gavel

Prisons under the Gavel

The Federal Court Takeover of Georgia Prisons

Bradley Stewart Chilton

Ohio State University Press
Columbus

K FG
588
C 48
1991

Library of Congress Cataloging-in-Publication Data

Chilton, Bradley Stewart. 1955–
    Prisons under the gavel : the federal court takeover of Georgia prisons / Bradley
Stewart Chilton.
      p. cm.
    Includes bibliographical references and index.
    ISBN 0-8142-0540-2 (alk. paper)
    1. Prisons—Law and legislation—Georgia. 2. Prisons—Law and legislation—
United States. 3. Prison administration—Georgia. 4. Prison administration—
United States. I. Title.
KFG588.C48   1991
344.758'035—dc20
[347.580435]   91-7941
                                                  CIP

The paper in this book meets the guidelines
for permanence and durability of the Committee
on Production Guidelines for Book Longevity
of the Council on Library Resources. ∞

Printed in the U.S.A.

9 8 7 6 5 4 3 2 1

To Lisa

Contents

Preface

The Longest Yard was a 1974 movie starring Burt Reynolds as a convict in a state prison in the Deep South. With a backdrop of stark white stucco prison buildings, the movie depicted the convict's struggle for dignity amidst the squalor and decay of a prison gone out of control. That backdrop was, in reality, the Georgia State Prison (GSP) in Reidsville, Georgia. This is a study of the *Guthrie v. Evans* lawsuit, which transformed GSP into a model constitutional prison.

Until the 1970s, judges played no more than a small role in the control and administration of prisons. They kept their hands off prison operations, and prisoners were treated as slaves of the state. Today, judicial intervention in correctional systems has become the norm as dozens of state prison systems and many local jails are under judicial scrutiny to change and improve the condition of life behind bars.

Judicial intervention in prisons and jails has sparked a great deal of controversy. Proponents of judicial activism and judicial restraint debate the constitutionality and effectiveness of prison reform litigation. However, philosophical debates over the legitimacy of judges intervening in prisons ought not be confused, as they often are, with empirical disputes over the capacity of judges to intervene in ways that make prisons and jails safer, more civilized, and more effective. We must recognize that judicial intervention in corrections is here to stay, and many prisons and jails have been greatly improved.

This exploratory study is aimed at identifying, in some systematic way, the political, administrative, budgetary, remedial, and other conditions that may help judges and other key decision-makers become more effective in the capacity to intervene in prison reform litigation. Specifically, in the protracted and complex interaction between a court (judge, special masters, and others) and the prison/state (wardens, lawyers, legislators, and executives), how does a case move from an initial petition to an outcome resulting in a dramatically altered prison environment? And what does this tell us about the jurisprudence of rights?

More broadly, I hope that those with no direct interest in the sub-

ject may learn something, too. First, of the tensions that arise in the
new partnership of the judiciary and public administrators. Second,
of the variety of leadership and organizational change as key decision-
makers must sometimes choose between a rock and a hard place.
Finally, of the validity of a practice of rights jurisprudence theory for
other areas of institution-wide reform by reference to constitutional
rights.

Acknowledgments

Thanks must first go to the lawyers, administrators, officials, inmates, guards, and judges whose cooperation made this research possible. I sought out and received their candid responses with the promise of anonymity. Particular thanks go to the Georgia attorney general, Michael Bowers, and assistant attorney general, John C. Jones, for use of the complete set of court documents of the *Guthrie* case from their files. Thanks also to Georgia Legal Services attorney Robert Cullen and Georgia Department of Corrections assistant commissioner Samuel W. Austin for other materials used in this research.

The intellectual heart of this book belongs to Susette M. Talarico, major professor of my dissertation committee. I had studied law and politics for some time before becoming one of Professor Talarico's students, and with her I was able to bring it all together for this exploratory research. Any insights found here can be traced back to our discourses. I also appreciate the detailed and illuminating direction given by dissertation committee members Loren Beth, Delmer Dunn, Thomas Lauth, and James Massey. Lief Carter, Phillip Cooper, Erica Fairchild, Malcolm Feeley, William Muir, Tinsley Yarbrough, and others contributed helpful suggestions at critical points in my research. With appreciation for the assistance of these many individuals, I stand alone in responsibility for this final product.

The collection of research data discussed in this book was partially funded by an American Judicature Society Dissertation and Law Review Research Grant, 1985–86. The collection of evidence, particularly news clippings, for this research would have been impossible without the cooperation of the staff at the Georgia Room Collection of the University of Georgia Libraries. Finally, I would like to thank my wife, Lisa Marie, who endured these many years of uncertainty and pressure with patient support and understanding. To her I give my love and many thanks.

1

Litigating Prison Reform

Guthrie v. Evans, Civil Action No. 73–3068, S.D. Ga. 1973, began and ended at the Georgia State Prison (GSP) in Reidsville, Georgia. It began with a four-page *in forma pauperis* (no fees required) complaint crudely written by inmates at the prison. But the lawsuit ended in a slick and shiny new hearing room at the renovated prison that symbolized the immense changes at the prison after many years of litigation. On Wednesday, June 26, 1985, in the hearing room at GSP, Judge Anthony A. Alaimo of the United States District Court for the Southern District of Georgia, Savannah Division, read a short statement that brought to an end the case that had been assigned to his docket thirteen years earlier. As the judge read the permanent injunction order, one could see through the clerestory window over his head to the upper floors of renovated inmate dormitories. Each statement of the order brought to mind the events in the saga of the reform of GSP: the renovated facilities; the many lawyers and court-appointed personnel; the moments of violence at GSP that made this case unlike any other. The judge read:

> The above case having come before the Court for the entry of a final judgment, having heard from counsel for both parties, it is hereby ORDERED, ADJUDICATED and ADJUDGED that the defendants, their agents, assigns, successors, employees and contractors are permanently enjoined from failing and refusing to comply with the orders entered in this case. The orders are set forth in the compendium, approved this date, the Georgia State Prison medical audit document, the Rogers Correctional Institution audit documents, stipulations and the other documents adopted or entered in this case as substantive orders of the Court. Failure to comply may result in a finding of contempt, imposition of fines and other appropriate remedies. The Orders on the protection afforded to confidential materials, protection

1

of witnesses, access to the prison by plaintiffs' counsel, discovery, and submission of proposed changes are specifically re-affirmed. The defendants shall continue to comply with each order and mandate issued in this case.

IT IS FURTHER ORDERED that defendants shall bear plaintiffs' prospective costs, expenses and attorneys' fees as they relate to defendants' requested changes of the permanent injunction of this case. However, plaintiffs' counsel shall submit a motion seeking recovery of fees, costs and expenses, and defendants shall retain the right to challenge the appropriateness of the number of hours expended and the rate sought. In the case of contempt litigation, plaintiffs must prevail in order to recover fees, costs and expenses for said litigation. In addition to the foregoing provisions relating to costs, fees and expenses, plaintiffs' counsel may, for a period of 12 months after the entry of this Order, and upon a proper showing and justification, file with the Court an application for the recovery of fees, costs and expenses for other matters involved in this case, to which defendants may raise any and all available defenses.

Guthrie v. Evans was over! After a brief moment of awkward silence, those in the hearing room broke into celebration with photos of the symbolic moment and a closing toast around a punch bowl. The reform of the Georgia State Prison was completed.

Prisons and Prison Reform

It is said that the prison is an American invention. Until the nineteenth century, places of imprisonment were used primarily to hold those awaiting trial, with the exception of certain political prisoners. However, prisons were in existence long before the American experiment in corrections (the Bridewell Palace in England was built in 1553 and the Milan, Italy, House of Correction in 1755). Even the underlying concept of the American prison as penitentiary was conceived in England by John Howard. In *The State of the Prisons in England and Wales, with Preliminary Observations, and an Account of Some Foreign Prisons,* published in 1777, Howard recorded the state of prisons in Europe and defined the prison in terms of a penitentiary. In such a prison, inmates were isolated from society and from each other so that they might do penance.

The American prison was born out of these reforms of the European prison system. Colonial America, like Europe at the time, seldom used prisons as punishment before the nineteenth century, except to hold the accused for trial. Instead, those convicted of crimes were subjected to indentured service, banishment, corporal punishment, the pillory, or death. But corrections reformers in the new nation set about to develop more humanistic treatment for those convicted of crimes. Pennsylvanians organized the Society for Alleviating the Miseries of Public Prisoners in 1787 under the leadership of Benjamin Franklin and the Quaker physician Dr. Benjamin Rush. This group pressured the Pennsylvania legislature to build Philadelphia's Walnut Street Jail, which was completed in 1790 and patterned after Howard's penitentiary. With the opening of Eastern State Penitentiary in 1829 the Pennsylvania system was characterized by the solitary confinement of each inmate.

Other systems, such as the New York System at Auburn, imitated the Pennsylvania system of isolation and penitence, in part by placing inmates in solitary confinement at night. The American penitentiary was quite an innovative reform of the European prisons and prompted Europeans such as Alexis de Tocqueville to travel through the United States to study them.

Since the birth of the penitentiary in America, reforms have continued to affect the corrections system, as leaders in corrections have developed new goals of punishment. The corporal and other punishments of colonial America exacted retribution of those convicted of crimes, and some theorists argued these punishments would deter others from crime. With a hope of rehabilitation through penitence, the early penitentiaries set as a goal the incapacitation of convicts. Later reformers grew disillusioned with the inhuman conditions that prevailed under the penitentiary model and developed the reformatory as a way of limiting these brutalities. With the reformatories came the rise of rehabilitation as a goal of punishment, starting with New York's Elmira Reformatory in 1876 and refined further through the 1970s. These progressive reforms included parole, probation, prison education and training, and individualized medical and psychological treatment. However, disillusionment with the rehabilitative model of punishment prevailed in the 1970s and continues today, as increasing numbers of inmates are shuttled off to isolated and overcrowded prisons that have become warehouses of human cattle to be kept off the streets (Sherman and Hawkins, 1981). In a sense, punishment in America has been reformed full circle back to the incapacitative goal of the early Pennsylvanians, except that today there is no longer the idealistic hope of reform through penitence in these warehouses.

Many of these reforms in corrections in America were traditionally identified, legitimated, and promulgated by executive and legislative officials. Reform governors, such as E. D. Rivers of Georgia in the 1930s, brought sweeping changes to the state corrections system to bring it up to date for their times. Reformers in the state and federal legislatures, particularly during the late nineteenth century, funded the necessary institution building or directed that the executive appoint wardens and other officials versed in the new correctional goals. But during most of American history, the courts adopted a hands-off policy toward the workings of the corrections system and the rights of those punished by these institutions. Inmates were said to be civilly dead—without civil rights while imprisoned. It was not until 1942 in *Cochran v. Kansas*, 316 U.S. 255 (1942), that the U.S. Supreme Court recognized that inmates had the right to appeal the conditions of their original conviction.

During the mid-1960s, however, courts at all levels abruptly became interested in the operations of correctional institutions and in the civil rights of the imprisoned. This hands-on phase quickly gave rise to court intervention in corrections activities not linked to specific inmates' rights, but generally affecting the conditions of their confinement. Class actions involving thousands of inmates statewide were considered by federal district court judges. These judges appeared to take over the responsibility of prison administration from the courthouse, especially as they mandated many details of day-to-day operations at prisons in judicial decrees. While this involvement by the courts has been more restrained since a series of important U.S. Supreme Court decisions in 1976, courts still provide the current leadership for prison reforms in America. These successful lawsuits—variously called extended impact litigation, complex litigation, structural reform litigation, public law litigation, and institutional reform litigation—sought not only to redress the individual civil rights violated by specific correctional activities, but to reform the entire corrections system in its conditions and procedures.

Institutional Reform Litigation

The application of constitutional rights to almost every aspect of the administrative state has become an important part of the day-to-day business of the courts. Courts have not only undertaken the reform of prisons, but also of mental institutions, public housing, public schools, and other public institutions. While on the surface these cases address the civil rights of specific individuals or groups, their impact is polycentric, as they also affect governmental institutions and personnel as well as many other citizens (Fuller, 1978). Plaintiffs who seek redress for an infraction of their civil rights by government authorities now more commonly seek structural changes in the governmental institutions themselves, not merely damages. In response, precise remedial decrees have been ordered specifying the protection of rights and structural changes in the institutions themselves. An unintended effect of this increased judicial supervision of governmental institutions has been to make the court an ally with the plaintiffs for administrative reforms (Rosenbloom, 1983). Thus, the courts have become reformers of governmental institutions by means of adversarial litigation, which is often accompanied by the resistance and delay common in trial procedures.

Institutional reform litigation can best be understood by comparison with conventional adjudication, as demonstrated in appendix D. Conventional adjudication is characterized by the filing of a complaint, followed by pre-trial discovery, trial or settlement, and a judgment by judicial decision or consent of the parties for damages. The issues are relatively narrow and concern one party suing another party over facts that occurred in the past. The one-time judgment is largely imposed by judicial decision but is applied only to the parties. Because it is expected that the judgment will be self-executing, little attention is paid to implementation. If the judgment is resisted, adversarial proceedings are initiated to obtain various judicial sanctions to compel performance.

Institutional reform litigation is likely to involve a far more complex process of pleadings in amendments to the complaints, extensive pre-trial discovery, and protracted hearings and trials. The parties may include thousands of named individuals in a class action lawsuit. The facts adduced at trial may include specific past violations of constitutional rights and predictive facts of what might happen to violate constitutional rights not yet legislated. The parties do not seek damages, but equitable remedies that will re-structure the governmental institution at fault by affirmative injunctions requiring positive action. In remedial decrees that are crafted after considerable negotiation, courts try to anticipate problems in implementation by specifying changes in detail and by providing the means to monitor compliance. The judge is less passive and considers issues from the entire political context of the government institution to help design and apply a remedy that will effect true change. Court-appointed special masters and monitors and other court-appointed experts assist the judge in assessing liability, crafting remedies, and measuring compliance, while the court retains jurisdiction over the case through to complete implementation.

With the proliferation of institutional reform litigation in prisons, attempts have been made to restrict or avoid the intrusion of lower federal courts in prison administration. Federal circuit courts of appeal have reversed lower court decisions that enjoin a jail from accepting any new prisoners until improved, *Rhem v. Malcolm*, 507 F. 2d 333 (2d Cir. 1974), and that dictate standards for future prison construction, *Williams v. Edwards*, 547 F. 2d 1206 (5th Cir. 1977). Even the Supreme Court has criticized lower courts for becoming too involved in the "minutiae of prison operations," *Bell v. Wolfish*, 99 S. Ct. 1861 (1979). Also, Congress and state legislatures have bills pending to restrict court jurisdiction and remedial powers in such cases (Nagel, 1984). Some prison administrators use alternatives to litigation to avoid court intrusions, with varying success. Alternatives such as inmate grievance procedures, ombudsmen, and legal assistance appear to succeed in reducing litigation, while mediation does not (Clear and Cole, 1986, pp. 460–66).

The Study of Prison Reform Litigation

How have scholars in law and the social sciences analyzed prison reform litigation in hopes of a systematic understanding of this form of judicial decision-making? To date, we can distinguish four major types of analyses. These include (1) macro-level analyses, (2) participant-observer analyses, (3) case studies, and (4) implementation or impact studies of prison reform litigation. We shall examine each in turn.

Macro-level Analyses focus on the capacity and legitimacy of courts as they address complex, polycentric, and protracted cases. These issues are discussed at length, often interminably. Without rich descriptions and by carefully selecting cases, both critics and supporters of court interventions are able to conclude for (e.g., Fiss, 1979) and against (e.g., Horowitz, 1978) court capacity to address the problems raised by prison reform litigation. Even more endless are the debates over the legitimacy of court intervention, with seemingly unresolvable normative argument over the appropriate judicial role (e.g., Chayes, 1976; Fiss, 1979; Glazer, 1978; Rosenbloom, 1988). While these debates may illuminate the normative reality of prison reform litigation, they argue normative claims that rest more on reactions to case results than court competence and frequently proceed without rich appreciation for specific cases.

Participant-Observer Analyses give valuable attention to the special problems that stem from actual experiences of participants in prison reform litigation. Some offer assurances that courts can and should do the tasks requested (Johnson, 1982; Justice, 1984). Other participants call for moderation of prison reform litigation (e.g., Brakel, 1986B). Participant-observer analyses exhibit a rich appreciation for actual cases and yield some understanding of the specific problems encountered (e.g., use of special masters: Brakel, 1986A; Nathan, 1979). Of course, they are suspect for bias. Furthermore, explications of selected problems leave much to be desired when compared against a systematic understanding of prison reform litigation.

Case Studies typically assess the degree of compliance by administrators at a specified point in time after court orders are issued. While some measure compliance or non-compliance, better studies measure compliance on a continuous scale reflecting degrees of partial compliance (e.g., Ball, Krane, and Lauth, 1982). Phillip Cooper (1988) labels these studies external, post-hoc and distinguishes the approach from his internal-dynamic case study method. The external, post-hoc approach focuses only on the actions and reactions of groups at some specified point after a court order and, thus, measures only compliance. Case studies of compliance, however, don't offer a systematic understanding of these litigation processes.

Cooper's internal-dynamic case study approach focuses on the perspectives (internal) of key decision-makers as they interact over time (dynamic) in the formulation and implementation of remedial decrees. Using this method, Cooper offers a rich description of several institutional reform lawsuits: *U.S. v. Parma*, 661 F. 2d 562 (6th Cir. 1981); *Milliken v. Bradley*, 418 U.S. 717 (1974) and 433 U.S. 267 (1977); *Wyatt v. Stickney*, 503 F. 2d 1305 (5th Cir. 1974); *Rhodes v. Chapman*, 452 U.S. 337 (1981); and *Rizzo v. Goode*, 423 U.S. 362 (1976). Cooper also presents a theoretical decree litigation model consisting of (1) a trigger phase (background from which the case arose), (2) a liability phase (establishing the existence, nature, and scope of the legal violation), (3) a remedy phase (decree is actually developed with parallel appeals), and (4) a post-decree phase (remedy is implemented, evaluated, and refined).

Implementation or Impact Studies do not provide systematic analyses of this variant of correction law, though one can find rich descriptions of particular cases. Field research of four prison totality of conditions cases, *Collins v. Schoonfield* (Baltimore City Jail), *Hamilton v. Schiro* (Orleans Parish Prison), *Holland v. Donelon* (Jefferson Parish Prison), and *Holt v. Sarver* (Arkansas State Penitentiary), details the extent of compliance with rich description of the many factors affecting remedial decree compliance. Examining the social and political climate, key participants' attitudes, and legal and administrative events of each case, Harris and Spiller (1976, pp. 21–29) conclude that compliance is largely due to background events, not to court intrusion. The courts provide the forum for public education about defects in the prison systems and create a climate for change.

However, these studies focus only on compliance. James Jacobs details the underlying problem with prison compliance studies: When and how can compliance be measured? Like others, Jacobs argues that we need to study the entire process of litigation and not only legal compliance. Specifically, Jacobs calls for an assessment of the way "the changing legal status of prisoners is reflected in social, political, and organizational change" (1981, p. 457).

To be sure, there are rich descriptions and some analyses of this litigation phenomenon. Excellent biographies and personality histories of those involved in such litigation (e.g., Yarbrough, 1981), as well as studies of the impact of this judicial intervention on state budgets (e.g., Taggart, 1989), are good examples. Analysis of legal variables has focused our attention on the nature of the core remedy

and key decision-maker position in understanding litigation perspectives (Cooper, 1988). But we are left with spotty and limited understanding of the actual process of prison reform litigation.

Richly descriptive studies of the impact of prison litigation have
recently appeared in print. Tinsley Yarbrough (1981; 1982; 1984;
1985) and Larry Yackle (1989) have written on the prison reform litigation in Alabama under Judge Frank Johnson. Other studies have
focused on the impact of the system-wide reform of Texas prisons
through litigation under Judge William Justice (DiIulio, 1987; Crouch
and Marquart, 1985; Martin and Ekland-Olson, 1987). This rich description and post-hoc analysis suggest several variables for inquiry.
These include key decision-makers' (1) personalities and interactions,
(2) perspectives on budgetary aspects, (3) perspectives on legal remedies and enforcement mechanisms, and (4) philosophical climate
involving changes in politics and corrections within a practice of
rights.

This work seeks systematically to understand the nature of prison
reform litigation in the context of the Guthrie case at the Georgia State
Prison in Reidsville, Georgia. The analysis relied on descriptions of
comparative cases in the literature and the archival data in Guthrie,
but most extensively on data gathered in focused interviews with key
decision-makers in Guthrie. Attention was focused on four important
and basic questions that arise from a rich case story of Guthrie. First,
who were the key decision-makers and how did they perceive the case
and underlying issues? Second, how did the budget for GSP change
in the course of litigation and what were the important factors in that
process? Third, what were the major remedies undertaken and how
did settlement patterns change in the course of the litigation? Finally,
what rights undergirded the Guthrie litigation and what does this tell
us about institutional reform litigation?

The discussion of our four questions renders new evidence and
analysis of widespread and growing litigation phenomena. Further
studies of prison reform litigation may benefit from clarification on
these basic questions by this rich empirical case description and analysis. For example, much of the literature that has developed around
prison reform litigation assumes that in such cases judges find violations of civil rights, design remedial decrees, mandate budgetary
changes, and actively participate in implementation. However, this
research reveals that in Guthrie, and in many other cases, these as-

sumptions are overly simplistic and false. More plausible explana-
tions of these litigation processes must go beyond the judge to include
all key decision-makers, as well as other factors.

The Institutionalization of Rights?

Meaning is given to values in law and equity through adjudication.
Courts give meaning by converting whatever is submitted to them for
decisions into claims of right or accusations of fault (Fuller, 1978).
Contemporary American jurisprudence includes three theories of the
nature of the interpretation of constitutional rights: adjudication of
pre-existing principle, adjudication by legislating policy, and adjudication as a practice of rights within a larger social organization.

While criticized by legal realists and judicial behavioralists, the
office of the judge as a neutral, objective, and rational adjudicator
of pre-existing principles is part of the accepted ideology of courts
(Scheingold, 1974). Ronald Dworkin (1978; 1985), as contemporary
spokesperson, affirms the unique role of courts in adjudicating principles, not policy, and posits an idealized Judge "Hercules" who can
find "one right answer" in every case, even with competing principles. Once the appropriate pre-existing principles are discovered and
applied to the case, the parties are rationally obliged to comply with
the court's judgment as they would to any contract (see also Rawls,
1971). In judicially managed institutional reform, Judge Hercules
seeks out and applies pre-existing constitutional principles that impose a burden of adequate custodial care on the state (Dworkin, 1985).

Dworkin's rights thesis, with its platitudes and idealized Judge
Hercules, fails to convince many that judges merely discover and
apply pre-existing principles. For example, David A. J. Richards
(1977, pp. 1096–1102) rebuts Dworkin's rights thesis and argues that
judges make policy decisions in this type of adjudication. As proof,
he demonstrates (1) that such decisions are granted to individuals
who cannot claim a right to the decision (e.g., Ernesto Miranda in
Miranda v. Arizona), (2) that decisions in these cases apply prospec-
tively and concern individuals whose rights were not presented or
even anticipated in court, and (3) that the courts develop policy even
in the "natural province of adjudication" (Richards, 1977, pp. 1096–
1102). A judge may formulate policy by economic, political, or other

criteria. Although Dworkin (1978; 1985) takes on these various policy criteria and faults an idealized Judge "Herbert" who adjudicates by legislating policy, his rights thesis gains no positive footing. This is disappointing, as his 1985 title promised needed attention to institutional reform litigation; specifically, it is named after a collection of Judge Frank Johnson's personal papers (*A Matter of Principle*). We are left only with Dworkin's earlier call (1978, p. 345) for research:

> This administrative business of courts, which Chayes thinks provides a new style of adjudication, raises a great many problems for jurisprudence and political theory . . . much more needs to be said about the energetic administrative role courts now seem to have assumed, and the impact of that practice on the rights thesis.

Others object to a rights thesis that idealizes adjudication by either a Hercules or a Herbert. From phenomenology, pragmatism, and Wittgensteinian linguistic analysis, Richard E. Flathman (1976) presents a theory of adjudication as a social practice of rights. As a framework for analysis, it promises a means of understanding, and accommodates both the individual and social dimensions of rights in a theory based on peoples' actions, not idealizations. Flathman introduces *The Practice of Rights* (1976, pp. 6, 17) accordingly:

> Rights arise out of and are accorded within a rule-governed social practice. But they are accorded to and exercised by individuals whose actions cannot be analyzed without significant remainder in terms of properties of the practice or the society more generally. Its aim is . . . to identify and give a systematic account and assessment of the assumptions, beliefs, ideas, values, expectations, and modes of action that are prominent in the practice as its participants understand it and engage in it.

Yarbrough's study (1981) of Judge Frank Johnson certainly seeks to understand institutional reform litigation from a participant's perspective. While critics fault Judge Johnson for imposing pure judicial will on the state of Alabama, Yarbrough (1981; 1982; 1985) presents a more systematic assessment of Judge Johnson and directs attention, in the process, to the practice of human rights in Alabama institutions. Negotiation and compromise, not the imperial judicial will of a Judge Hercules or Herbert, characterize the practice of rights in institutional reform litigation. In this instance, the judge perceives his/her role as a catalyst (Moss, 1985) or powerbroker (Diver, 1979), presiding over a negotiation process and pushing administrators, attorneys, and legislators in a general direction to institutional reform. Changing social forces, politics, legal mandates, attorneys' imaginations, and the science of corrections, as well as litigation costs and duration, frustrate a judge from exercising "pure will" (Yarbrough, 1982; 1985). This set of social conditions and interactions comes to define the practice of rights that make up a constitutional prison.

Adjudication as a practice of rights may provide a theory of jurisprudence to justify the current use of prison reform litigation. The adjudication of individual rights is transformed into a discourse between a large number of key decision-makers, such as attorneys, special masters and monitors, prison experts, wardens, and others. In so doing, the central question changes from "What inmates' rights are being violated?" to "What is a constitutional prison?" Thus, judges have a solid claim to the capacity to undertake institution-wide reform by working within a larger social organization of key decision-makers to resolve these cases. But the question remains: what are the consequences of the institutionalization of individual constitutional rights?

Chapters 2 through 5 present a chronological history of the events in the *Guthrie* lawsuit, divided into four phases: trigger, liability, remedy, and post-decree (Cooper, 1988). Chapters 6 and 7 distill the events of the lawsuit into four sets of factors that may help to explain the nature of the *Guthrie* litigation in particular and institutional reform litigation in general. These include the interacting personalities and perspectives of key decision-makers, budgetary politics, remedial decree designs, and the nature of the interpretation of constitutional rights. Finally, chapter 8 provides a critique of the institutionalization of rights in prison reform litigation, a comparison of these findings, and the extant literature on other prison reform cases. In addition, various appendixes list the sources of evidence used in the study of *Guthrie*, describe the methodology used, and illustrate the extent of prison reform cases in the United States today.

2

The Emergence of *Guthrie*

Over seventeen years have passed since federal courts first intervened in prison operations at the Georgia State Prison in Reidsville, Georgia, under the *Guthrie* case. On September 29, 1972, Arthur S. Guthrie, Joseph Coggins II, and fifty other black inmates of GSP signed a four-page *in forma pauperis* complaint to federal courts that led to the most detailed and comprehensive set of remedial decrees ever imposed on a single prison facility (Pollock, 1983). Judge Anthony A. Alaimo of the U.S. District Court for the Southern District of Georgia officially sanctioned the lawsuit, which has been variously titled *Guthrie v. MacDougall, Guthrie v. Caldwell, Guthrie v. Ault*, and *Guthrie v. Evans*. Judge Alaimo was the catalyst for changes in prison sanitation, food preparation, temperature control, fire control, industries, and ventilation. He also mandated inmate classification, racial desegregation, overcrowding restrictions, security segregation, disciplinary procedures, grievance procedures, religious freedoms, security, safety, visitation privileges, law library access, exercise privileges, rehabilitation, educational programs, and medical, dental, and mental health programs (Department of Offender Rehabilitation, 1982). Judge Alaimo terminated nearly thirteen years' involvement in *Guthrie* with a final injunctive order on June 26, 1985.

Chapters 2 through 5 outline the development of the *Guthrie* case. Data for this study were gathered by direct observations of proceedings, interviews with key decision-makers, and archival analysis of relevant court records, monitors' reports, the U.S. Civil Rights Commission study of Georgia prisons, departmental, legislative, and gubernatorial reports, other relevant court decisions, and various newspaper and news magazine reports. As explained earlier, this chronology of *Guthrie* is modeled on Cooper's (1988) four phases of institutional reform litigation: trigger, liability, remedy, and post-decree.[1]

The Legal Basis of Prison Reform Litigation

The Eighth Amendment of the U.S. Constitution expressly protects those convicted of a crime by prohibiting excessive punishment, including "cruel and unusual punishment." In recent decades, the civil rights enumerated in the Constitution have been increasingly used for prison reform by courts. In the 1960s and 1970s, courts expanded their involvement in reforming prison practices and conditions, and emphasized that prison inmates possessed civil rights found in the First, Fourth, Fifth, Sixth, Eighth, and Fourteenth amendments. This expansion now permits a wide range of prison conditions and practices to rise as constitutional violations under civil rights provisions on religion, communication, searches, due process of law, access to the courts, punishment, and equal protection of the law. *Trop v. Dulles*, 356 U.S. 86, at 101 (1958), makes this explicit, establishing "evolving standards of decency" as the test of unconstitutional prison conditions and practices. With this subjective standard, lower courts can, and sometimes do, scrutinize almost every phase of prison operations.

The use of civil rights for prison reform was expanded by the courts' use of prison inmate class action lawsuits under 42 U.S.C. 1983 and its jurisdictional counterpart, 28 U.S.C. 1343 (3), (4); 2201 and 2202. Many improper prison practices or conditions with individual inmates do not reach a constitutional level and are considered trivial. Under a Section 1983 class action, these individual instances can be combined with those of a group of inmates complaining of a totality of conditions that creates an institution-wide prison environment in violation of the Constitution (Low and Jeffries, 1988). This post–Civil War statute (1871) provides:

> Every person who, under color of any statute, ordinance, regulation, custom, or usage, of any State or Territory, subjects, or causes to be subjected, any citizen of the United States or other person within the jurisdiction thereof to the deprivation of any rights, privileges, or immunities secured by the Constitution and laws, shall be liable to the party injured in an action at law, suit in equity, or other proper proceeding for redress.

As a type of institutional reform litigation, this kind of prison reform lawsuit began in Arkansas, Mississippi, and Alabama in the 1960s and has grown to include prisons in thirty-eight states.

As traditional neutral arbiters, judges were reluctant to interfere in the administration of prisons. But where the totality of conditions violated the Eighth Amendment so egregiously, federal court judges did not hesitate to do whatever had to be done to remedy the situation. For example, Judge Frank Johnson removed control of prisons from the Alabama corrections system and placed them into direct receivership, with the governor as receiver (Yarbrough, 1981).

Trigger Phase: 1933–73

The trigger phase includes the fact pattern or background from which *Guthrie* emerged, until it was officially sanctioned by the federal court as a federal class action lawsuit. The transformation of an ordinary civil rights dispute to institutional reform litigation necessarily includes many diverse events that occurred over decades of an institution's history. Thus, it is necessary to begin with trigger events that happened long before Arthur S. Guthrie came on the scene.

Prison reforms in Georgia seem to follow crises. When the state's first penitentiary, built in 1817, was burned in General William Sherman's march to the sea in 1864, Georgia developed the convict lease system as a way to detain penitents without a penitentiary in the impoverished state economy. The state received $11.00 per annum for each convict. However, the cruelty and graft of the lease system were uncovered years later and brought to an end by the state in 1899. In that year, the General Assembly ordered that all state prisoners be maintained on state prison farms or county road gangs. Thus, the era of the chain gangs began. Georgia later became known as the chain gang capital of the United States. At one work camp, the Rock Quarry Prison, inmates would break their own legs with sledgehammers to avoid "bustin' rock" on an unending rock pile. Public outrage and a reform governor, E. D. Rivers, put an end to chain gangs in 1937.

Much of the outrage was generated by the story of one prisoner. In 1931, Robert Elliot Burns wrote a book, *I Am a Fugitive from a Georgia Chain Gang,* which was made into a movie the following year. Burns told of inhumanities in the Georgia prison system, from which he escaped twice. Burns described himself as a jobless and hungry World War I veteran who in 1922 accompanied a flophouse acquaintance in the robbery of a grocery store that netted five dollars. He was captured, sentenced to six to ten years, and placed on a chain gang working the roads. He escaped after two months and fled to Chicago, where he became a successful, $20,000-a-year magazine editor. In 1929, his first wife told authorities of his whereabouts, and he was returned to Georgia and the chain gang. Burns escaped again the following year, went to New Jersey, and wrote the book. Three New Jersey governors refused to extradite him to Georgia after Burns became a respected tax consultant in Newark. Governor Eugene Talmadge and other Georgia officials called Burns's story untrue, but in 1937 Governor E. D. Rivers ordered chain gangs eliminated.[2] Later governors abolished all use of leg irons, chains, and manacles, as well as striped uniforms and the use of whips in state prisons.

The Georgia State Prison was started in 1933, according to a contract by which the U.S. government would erect the prison building and the state of Georgia would pay, over a period of years, 70 percent of the cost of the project (including interest). The U.S. government made a grant to the state of 30 percent of the project cost. First, 980 acres adjoining state land in Tattnall County, Georgia (on the Ohoopee River) were purchased and set aside for the project. The lowest bidder for the prison buildings was the Struck Construction Company of Louisville, Kentucky, at $1,083,000. The Stewart Iron Works Company of Cincinnati, Ohio, and Covington, Kentucky, was the lowest bidder on jail equipment at $198,980. The total cost was $1,281,980. The cornerstone was laid in 1936, and the project was completed within the limits of the contracts by January 1, 1937 (*Atlanta Journal*, 1/10/37). Governor E. D. Rivers emphasized that the new facility was the most expensive public building in the state of Georgia, costing even more to construct than the state capitol building (Rivers, 1938).

Inspired by successful facilities for youthful offenders, GSP featured a telephone-pole design with rows of open dormitories linked by a long central corridor. It originally measured approximately 1,020 feet along the front by 842 feet deep and contained eight inmate units designed to hold two thousand prisoners. Touted as the Alcatraz of the Piney Woods, it was surrounded by facilities for the inmates, including two large recreation fields (each 450 feet by 600 feet), small exercise yards, and industrial and agricultural work areas. A sculptural panel over the main entrance, by Julian Harris of Atlanta, depicted the anticipated inmate activities in agriculture and industry. The main building housed prison administrators and death row. Dormitory units on the right side of the main building housed white male inmates, while those on the left housed black male inmates. There were four complete mess halls for the white inmates and two separate mess halls for the black inmates. Further, "young boys" were separated from "more hardened types of criminals" (Rivers, 1938). The prison came to be known as Reidsville because of its location six miles from that city.

Over the next few decades, state authorities granted GSP a degree of deference not given other correctional facilities. Under the leadership of strong wardens such as Robert P. Balkcom,[3] GSP emerged as a self-sufficient prison community requiring no state funds for its operations. GSP was praised by the state legislature for its excellent conditions. The massive farm operations and strict discipline produced a profit, which also served to insulate GSP from state and federal scrutiny. The warden needed none of the government's monetary support; thus, it presented no meaningful threat to the exercise of his power.

This insulation from state or federal monies also isolated GSP from changes in penology. GSP continued practices of racial segregation, corporal discipline, and forced labor unchecked by outside authorities. GSP also used the hole: a small, dark, bedless and windowless room for solitary confinement of troublesome inmates, who were often placed there naked, without toiletries, for up to thirty days on a diet of bread and water with one full meal every fifth day. Medical facilities were characterized as a modern equivalent of a medieval pest house, and one GSP medical director was accused of privately selling blood donated by inmates. The one outside review of GSP—part of a 1963 statewide review by Illinois penologist Joseph E. Ragen—expressed alarm at the overcrowding and disciplinary practices at GSP and recommended specific changes. However, administrators, guards, and inmates alike resisted reforms. Warden Balkcom blamed the policy changes recommended by Ragen for the prison riot on September 4, 1963, which involved approximately two thousand inmates and resulted in thirty-five injuries.

In 1968, the long history of racial segregation in Georgia prisons was successfully challenged by sixteen civil rights leaders, including Hosea L. Williams, Sam W. Williams, Jesse Hill, Jr., and former inmates Phil Whitus and Leon Davis. This biracial group argued for an end to racial discrimination against inmates in all Georgia prisons, and asked the court to require that the state hire more "Negro law-men" and abolish all county work camps. Georgia Attorney General Arthur K. Bolton argued that the plaintiffs had no standing since "not one of the plaintiffs alleged he had ever sought employment as a prison guard or sheriff's deputy." In *Wilson v. Kelley*, 294 F. Supp. 1005 (N.D. Ga. 1968), the three-judge federal district court in Atlanta ordered the desegregation of all state prisons in Georgia, including Reidsville. Judges Sidney O. Smith, Jr., and Frank Hooper, however, declined without comment the other matters alleged by the plaintiffs. Judge Tuttle dissented on the decision not to address the job discrimination issue.

Georgia Governor Lester Maddox decried the three-judge court decree, arguing that desegregation would bring greater violence to state prisons. He was very critical of the plaintiffs and American Civil Liberties Union representatives in the case:

> [O]ur problem is already a difficult one without directions from the enemies of this country. They have not been satisfied that their previous decisions and actions as demanded by Socialists and Communists brought the rioting, looting, wrecking and assassination to this country. It seems that the Socialists and Communists in this Country and those who fight for the Socialist and Communist in the Country are not going to be satisfied until they control every baby bed, every hospital bed, every church, every school. (*Gainesville Daily Times*, 6/28/68)

However, on January 7, 1969, Governor Maddox asked the state legislature for funds to phase out the state's sixty-five public work camps.

On December 16, 1968, the U.S. Supreme Court affirmed the order and called for immediate desegregation plans by January 1, 1969, in *Wilson v. Kelley*, 294 F. Supp. 1005, aff'd., 393 U.S. 266 (1968). Supreme Court Justices Byron White and William Douglas dissented in part, indicating that the remainder of the case ought to be heard. The desegregation order took effect on January 1, 1969, and was often referred to as the 1969 order. Eventually, the segregated east and west wings of GSP were replaced by a checkerboard pattern of black and white dormitories along the central corridor, with alternate use of dining facilities. But there was no real racial integration within each dormitory.

When James E. Carter took control of the Georgia governor's office

in 1970, a top priority was to gain control of the state prison system. He appointed Ellis MacDougall chief of the system on February 1, 1970, and set about to create what was to be called the Department of Offender Rehabilitation (DOR). MacDougall and Carter
agreed the biggest problem would be GSP: it served as a breeding
ground for violence and the administrators and guards seemed resis-
tant to change.

     MacDougall began by appointing a new warden. On April 1, 1971,
"Jack" E. B. Caldwell replaced S. Lamont Smith. Caldwell had over
eighteen years' experience in corrections. He previously served as
superintendent of the Georgia Diagnostic and Classification Center in
Jackson (1970–71), and as warden at the Georgia Industrial Institute at
Alto (1969–70). A native of Upson, Georgia, Caldwell had attended
the universities of Georgia and Southern Illinois and the Woodrow
Wilson College of Law in Atlanta, and had served as the chief institu-
tional parole officer for the Georgia State Pardon and Parole Board.
His brother, Johnnie Caldwell, was the state comptroller general.
Caldwell's prime goals were more correctional officers, counselors,
and educational programs for inmates.

     The physical facilities at GSP in 1970 had changed little since
1937. The dormitories were grossly overcrowded and impossible to
patrol by guards who feared for their lives. The prison was understaffed, with only 166 correctional officers or about 40 per shift for
over 2,500 inmates. Governor Carter obtained $417,000 in federal
grant money to relieve overcrowding at GSP, but it was only seed
money for the necessary capital improvements.

     Although GSP had developed without the need of outside state or
federal funding and was self-sufficient due to the profits of its farm
operations, the prison was now burdened with lower productivity,
lower agriculture prices, overcrowding, and a neglected physical
facility. State legislators were not willing to spend scarce state funds
on convicted felons when schools and universities were in need. It
was a political stalemate. MacDougall warned that the situation at
GSP was breeding violence, complaining, "We don't run that prison—
the prisoners do. Whether you exist in that dormitory depends on how
strong and violent you are" (Atlanta Constitution, 11/30/71).

     In May 1972, the transfer of fifty elderly inmates (twenty-five black,
twenty-five white) from GSP to Milledgeville, Georgia, apparently
caused a race riot at GSP between white and black inmates, many of

whom were seriously injured. To relieve tensions, DOR Commissioner MacDougall ordered the immediate segregation of all inmate quarters at GSP, violating the 1969 order requiring desegregation. However, MacDougall promised to re-integrate the prison.

On September 29, 1972, *Coggins & Guthrie v. Caldwell* was initiated by Joseph Coggins II, Arthur S. Guthrie, and fifty other black inmates of GSP. The *in forma pauperis* motion and complaint were filed with the United States District Court for the Northern District of Georgia, Atlanta, Georgia. The inmates initiated the 42 U.S.C. 1983 civil rights class action lawsuit under the jurisdiction of 28 U.S.C. 1343 and the Eighth and Fourteenth amendments of the U.S. Constitution. The plaintiffs sought no monetary damages but only equitable relief for alleged illegal actions perpetrated against them. Warden Caldwell and "the Georgia Board of Corrections, Et-Al" were the named defendants.

The complaint, a four-page typed document, listed First, Fifth, Eighth, and Fourteenth Amendment violations. The complaint stated the duties of Warden E. B. Caldwell and the Georgia Board of Corrections were to "discharge all custodial and correctional duties of . . . Georgia State Prison" and to care for "the welfare (both medical and general) and safety of inmates of said prison." Furthermore, it alleged that these duties were constitutionally breached by (1) racial segregation of living and dining quarters, (2) denial of mailing rights to inmates writing their relatives (including censorship and seizure of mail received from relatives), (3) denial of visitation, and (4) racial discrimination in civilian employment at GSP (allegedly, there were only two blacks among one thousand employees). The plaintiff-inmates recounted specific incidents of constitutional violations for each allegation, but did not identify the injured inmates by name. In their appeal to the court, the plaintiff-inmates asked for the court's permission to file *in forma pauperis*, and for desegregation, better mailing and visiting privileges, more black civilian employees at GSP, and "all further relief as the court may deem proper and just."

Other inmate class action lawsuits were filed during this time and later merged with the case known as *Guthrie*. These included *Watson & Brewster v. Caldwell*, *Mullen v. Caldwell*, *Lee & Russell v. Mac-Dougall*, and *Simmons v. MacDougall*. Inmate James Watson (of *Watson & Brewster*) was the first to sign the *Coggins & Guthrie* complaint. Similarities between the two cases and a prior friendship between

Guthrie and Watson suggested some pooling of knowledge and re-sources by plaintiff-inmates. *Watson & Brewster* involved forty-two black inmates complaining of Fifth, Eighth, and Fourteenth Amendment violations at GSP and was officially merged with *Guthrie* on November 11, 1974. *Mullen* involved a complaint by six Black Muslims alleging constitutional violation of religious freedoms by GSP authorities and was merged by court order into *Guthrie* on November 6, 1973. The *Lee & Russell* and *Simmons* cases were filed at a later time against the commissioner of the Georgia Department of Rehabilitation, but were merged by the court with *Guthrie*.

Joseph Coggins II was a black inmate of GSP convicted of robbery in Clarke County, Georgia, on September 4, 1970. However, after two years, Coggins's case was retried and he was released to Clarke County, Georgia, on December 7, 1972. His 1970 sentencing hearing apparently included evidence of Coggins's previous criminal convictions obtained in cases where he had no lawyer. He was released December 29, 1972, to the Queens County, New York, House of Detention for other charges pending there. Because he was no longer in Georgia custody, and upon motion filed on behalf of Warden E. B. Caldwell, Coggins was dropped from the suit on May 15, 1973, as moot.

Arthur Samuel Guthrie, GSP #D-6978, was a black inmate with twelve misdemeanor and three felony convictions (before September 1972), including burglary, escape, robbery, and "flimflam." At the time the lawsuit was initiated, he was serving a life sentence at GSP on a Fulton County, Georgia, murder conviction (10/27/70). Guthrie had met Watson (of *Watson & Brewster v. Caldwell*) at the Fulton County Jail before being transferred to GSP. Because Coggins was moot in the case after his transfer out of Georgia, Guthrie's name was used after May 15, 1973, to identify the case.

The clerk of the United States District Court, Northern District of Georgia, Atlanta Division, received the *in forma pauperis* motion and complaint on October 2, 1972, and docketed the case with Judge Albert J. Henderson, Jr. Judge Henderson construed the case to be seeking "declaratory and injunctive relief for themselves and all other black inmates at the Reidsville prison facility" concerned with "numerous acts of racial discrimination against black inmates." In an order of October 26, 1972, he allowed the plaintiff-inmates to proceed *in forma pauperis* and ordered the named defendants or their legal representatives to respond or answer the complaint. The *Atlanta Jour-*

nal (10/28/72) reported the case as "State Prison Inmates Sue For Integration." It reported that DOR Commissioner MacDougall announced "plans are proceeding to re-integrate the Reidsville facility," yet inmates complained of segregated living quarters, inadequate mailing and visitation privileges, and racial discrimination in civilian hiring.

Georgia Attorney General Arthur K. Bolton was contacted on October 31, 1972 by defendant Ellis C. MacDougall, officially requesting representation. Warden Caldwell's request followed on November 8, 1972. Bolton, a native of Griffin, Georgia, and graduate of the University of Georgia law school, assigned the case to the criminal division and Assistant Attorney General Dorothy T. Beasley. Beasley worked on a strategy with Warden Caldwell to quickly resolve the matter and avoid a costly jury trial. The first step was a motion to dismiss (11/20/72) that contested jurisdiction of a 42 U.S.C. 1983 action against the Georgia Board of Corrections or against Warden Caldwell, who resided in the Southern District of Georgia. Although signed by Arthur K. Bolton and assistant attorneys general Harold N. Hill, Jr., Courtney Wilder Stanton, and Dorothy T. Beasley, the document directed all service to Beasley, who was clearly in charge of the case. The plaintiff-inmates denied all allegations in the motion to dismiss and moved for summary judgment in their favor on November 24, 1972.

Meanwhile, a Columbus, Georgia, attorney named Sanford D. Bishop, Jr., received a call from the NAACP Legal Defense Fund in New York in late November. The fund had received a letter from Joseph Coggins complaining of racial segregation, poor conditions, use of force, discrimination in parole, mail inspection, and inadequate medical care at GSP. The NAACP asked if Bishop were willing to talk with Coggins to see if there were some basis to his claims. Bishop, a native Georgian and graduate of Morehouse College, was an Earl Warren Fellow at Emory Law School from 1968 to 1971 (the fellowship was established to assist minority law students attending white law schools in the south). Bishop worked in New York for one year in civil rights litigation from 1971 to 1972 and agreed to return to the south to practice law and take NAACP cases in Georgia for three years. In Georgia, Bishop worked with Ralph Hudlin, Herbert Phipps, and Henrietta Turnquest. As an Earl Warren Fellow, Bishop agreed to talk with Coggins.

Coggins & Guthrie presented substantial difficulties from the start.

Shortly after Bishop notified Judge Henderson that he might be on the case (12/1/72), inmate Coggins was transferred to Clarke County and then to New York (12/7/72, 12/29/72). Bishop complained that he wasn't allowed into the prison to see Coggins; he then found that Coggins had been transferred out of the state. Bishop decided to take the case and began to prepare a motion to amend the complaint.

On January 31, 1973, before Bishop could file his motion, Judge Henderson dismissed the inmates' complaint for lack of jurisdiction. He reasoned that "every person" referred to in 42 U.S.C. 1983 didn't include a state or government agency, so the suit could be brought only against those exercising "day-to-day supervision and control of the prisoners and plaintiffs." Furthermore, he asserted, the Eleventh Amendment prohibits citizens from suing a state without the state's consent. Only Warden Caldwell was a proper defendant as a day-to-day supervisor at GSP, but the court held no personal jurisdiction over him since he resided outside the Northern District, and the complaint was dismissed. Assistant Attorney General Beasley was happily surprised with the result: could all GSP inmate lawsuits be dismissed against the state and central agency, with only the warden as the proper defendant?

The next six months were critical in transforming *Guthrie* from a simple *in forma pauperis* complaint to a class action lawsuit. Rather than order a new lawsuit, Judge Henderson transferred the original complaint to the Southern District of Georgia. The case was assigned to Judge Anthony A. Alaimo. Alaimo was born in 1920 in Termini, Sicily, Italy, and immigrated as a child with his parents to the United States. He grew up in Ohio, graduating with a bachelor of arts degree from Ohio Northern University before World War II (1940). He served as a 1st Lieutenant with the U.S. Army Air Corps from 1942 to 1946, and was captured and placed in a German prisoner of war camp in northern Italy near the Swiss border. He was decorated for his heroic escape when, disguised as an Italian worker, he went to Switzerland. In 1948, he earned the J.D. degree from Emory University in Atlanta, Georgia, and was admitted to the Georgia Bar. Appointed by President Nixon to the federal District Court for the Southern District of Georgia on December 9, 1971, Alaimo became chief judge in 1979.

The parties took a more adversarial posture over the next six months. Edith Burden, Georgia commissioner to the U.S. Civil Rights

Commission, called in the Civil Rights Division of the U.S. Department of Justice. The defendants, in turn, contacted the Augusta, Georgia, FBI office to inspect GSP. Previously told by headquarters "not to mess with GSP," the local office did not know the case was in court, but inspected the prison on March 22, 1973, upon defendants' request. Inmate Guthrie refused to discuss the case with Warden Caldwell, saying, "I ain't tellin' y'all a God damn thing!" Later, after Judge Alaimo signed a deposition order (5/15/73), Guthrie still refused to talk under orders from his attorneys, who had instructed him in a telegram, "Do not submit to any oral deposition on 7/3 or any other day unless hear from Bishop." This was particularly trying on defendants' attorney Beasley, who was alerted at the airport just before flying to Reidsville with a court reporter. When the deposition finally came together on July 5, 1973, Guthrie said very little. His attorneys filed motions that he be allowed to deposition Warden Caldwell and assistant wardens.

Assistant Attorney General Beasley worked through several strategies with others in the attorney general's office to narrow or circumvent the lawsuit. No one in the office wanted a prison conditions suit like those in Alabama, Arkansas, or Louisiana. At first, simple consolidation of *Guthrie* with the 1969 desegregation order in *Wilson v. Kelley* seemed an easy solution; *Guthrie* just contested how prison officials at GSP carried out the 1969 order. Quickly, however, the issues in *Guthrie* grew beyond segregation. As Judge Alaimo granted federal habeas corpus (5/2/73), plaintiffs' attorneys filed an extensively revised, twenty-five-page complaint claiming constitutional violations in GSP prison conditions, medical services, isolated confinement and visitation policies, use of mails, and disciplinary and rehabilitative practices, as well as racial discrimination. The new complaint also named Commissioner Ellis MacDougall and members of the Offender Rehabilitation and Corrections boards as additional defendants. The strategy for the Georgia attorney general's office then became one of scrapping over each clause of the new complaint: class action status, factual denials, and requiring a new suit.

Counsel for plaintiff-inmates now included active representation from members of the NAACP Legal Defense Fund, including Lynn Walker, Marilyn J. Holifield, and Charles S. Ralston. Ralston, a 1963 graduate of Boalt Hall School of Law (University of California, Berkeley) and first assistant counsel at LDF, supervised the activities of

Walker, Holifield, and Bishop in the case. Marilyn Holifield, a graduate of Swarthmore College and Harvard Law School, prepared to litigate the case. Walker traveled to GSP and got eleven of the original
fifty-two inmates to sign attorney retainer forms with the LDF. Bishop
pressed with the amended complaint; while Holifield and Walker
followed with a barrage of motions for class action status (6/28/73), to
produce documents (7/2/73), for a pre-trial conference (7/2/73), and
for twenty-five plaintiff-inmates (7/6/73) and four inmate-witnesses
to appear in court (7/9/73).

Judge Alaimo granted federal habeas corpus on May 2, 1973, and
scheduled a hearing in the Brunswick, Georgia, federal district court
building on July 10, 1973. Ruling that Joseph Coggins was moot as a
plaintiff, Alaimo pressed for a full evidentiary hearing to take care of
the matter with Arthur S. Guthrie, which he perceived as allegations
of specific legal injuries. However, he quickly realized that the case
had grown beyond these limits with the intense struggle over the
amended complaint and following motions. Alaimo notified the parties that the July 10 hearing was to rule on the motions and schedule
pre-trial discovery. He also decided that only two or three inmates
would be allowed in the courtroom, and that any future hearings
would be conducted at GSP.

The July 10 hearing was a watershed for the plaintiff-inmates, represented by attorneys Bishop, Holifield, and Hudlin. Not only did
Judge Alaimo orally grant their motion to file the new amended complaint, but he orally granted class action status and a pre-trial conference, and added new defendants. The defendants, represented by
Dorothy Beasley, won certain points when the judge required one
change in the amended complaint and denied inmate depositions
of Warden Caldwell and assistant wardens Phillip Seay and Bruce
Brown (security and medical care). Furthermore, certain key documents were protected from plaintiffs' discovery for reasons of GSP
security. But Georgia now had a "big prison case" like other states:
Guthrie v. MacDougall, as a discussion of the similarities of *Guthrie*
with *Watson & Brewster v. Caldwell*, hinted that Judge Alaimo would
merge other GSP cases into a single case. The judge orally instructed
the defendants to submit by July 16, 1973, a proposed class action
notice to all GSP inmates.

Plaintiffs' counsel filed the amended complaint on July 23, 1973,
with the one change Alaimo had discussed at the hearing. But attor-

ney Bishop was concerned with the substance and procedure of the defendants' proposed notice, and with improper pressures brought against inmates by prison officials and counselors who would attempt to maintain "the conditions complained of" by promising early release to inmates not participating in "trouble lawsuits." Judge Alaimo disagreed, arguing that Bishop should not "overlook pressures, subtle or otherwise, exerted by plaintiffs to include members of a proposed class. In matters of this nature, pressures are not unilateral."

The class action pleadings were formally ordered on August 10, 1973, although granted orally by Judge Alaimo at the July 10 hearing. The proposed class was defined by Judge Alaimo to include "all black inmates of the Georgia State Prison, Reidsville, Georgia, who do not expressly request to be excluded." The defendants' proposed notice of the lawsuit was approved and posted on all bulletin boards at GSP, as well as given to all GSP counselors to read to inmates. The notice included a summary of (1) the defined class and exclusion from the class (and no money damages), (2) the substance of the suit, (3) the right to read or have the complaint read, and (4) the requirement of posting the notice. With the execution of this notice, the class action pleadings were certified on August 13, 1973. In 1983, the defined class was expanded to include all GSP inmates, white and black, since the class action was certified in 1973:

> All present and future inmates incarcerated in the Georgia State Prison at Reidsville, Georgia, and all inmates incarcerated at the Georgia State Prison at Reidsville, Georgia, since April 15, 1974 . . . redefined to more precisely encompass the actual class membership . . . it has consistently been the parties' intent and practice to implement the orders entered in this action for the benefit of all inmates equally.

3

Determining Liability in *Guthrie*

Liability Phase: 1973–1979

During the liability phase, participants litigate the existence, scope, and nature of legal violations requiring legal and/or equitable relief. Although *Guthrie* was initiated by an informal association of concerned black inmates, it was quickly taken over by Bishop and the NAACP Legal Defense Fund attorneys. Events in this and later phases of *Guthrie* were dominated by attorneys, with the plaintiff-inmates as quiet and sometimes silent partners.

The liability phase of *Guthrie* was unusually long and complex in comparison with other prison reform lawsuits. Litigation over the scope and nature of violations at GSP began in 1973 and ended with the final report of hearings on October 8, 1979. In contrast, the Mississippi prison case *Gates v. Collier*, 423 F. Supp. 732 (N.D. Miss. 1974), was filed in February 1972, with a decision by the court on September 13, 1972.

An underlying step prior to the liability phase period was a department-wide reorganization of DOR and removal of Warden E. B. Caldwell from GSP. Caldwell was promoted to deputy commissioner on August 1, 1973, and was replaced by Joseph S. Hopper, who would head GSP for the next five years. Hopper had been deputy warden while Caldwell was warden at GSP.

The filing of plaintiffs' "First Amended Complaint for Injunctive and Declaratory Relief" on July 23, 1973, clearly defined the controversy. It proceeded as a class action pursuant to Rule 23 of the Federal Rules of Civil Procedure, under jurisdiction of 28 U.S.C. sections 1331 and 1343. The complaint asked for a preliminary and permanent injunction directing defendants to cease violating the rights of plaintiffs. Facts of violative prison conditions and practices were described in detail. These included housing conditions, food and its distribution, prison discipline and punishment, visitation privileges, inmate mail and literature, staff training and qualifications, lack of treatment programs, unresponsiveness to and reprisals for voiced grievances, and racial discrimination. Violations of various constitutional amendments were claimed, including cruel and unusual punishment (Eighth), right to privacy (Ninth), due process of law (Fifth and Fourteenth), racial discrimination (Fourteenth), right to counsel (Sixth), right to association (First), freedom of speech (First), and the right of human beings to be treated with dignity and decency (Ninth and Fourteenth). Plaintiffs further alleged that these violations were systemic and asked for remedies under 42 U.S.C. sections 1981, 1983, 1985, and 1994. The prayer for relief in the complaint asked the court to allow plaintiffs to proceed *in forma pauperis* and as a class action, declare and enjoin the defendants from violating plaintiffs' rights, direct defendants to submit a remedial plan, order affirmative action in hiring at GSP, retain jurisdiction over defendants to ensure implementation, and grant plaintiffs' costs of the suit and attorneys' fees. It was signed by Bishop and Holifield as attorneys for plaintiffs.

The defendants filed answers that argued that the plaintiffs "failed to state a claim upon which relief can be granted" and asked for a jury trial. Defendants also filed a motion to dismiss claims against Commissioner MacDougall and the DOR board members because they had "no authority or responsibility regarding the administration of the Georgia State Prison." Ralph Hudlin, Jr., as Bishop's law partner and plaintiffs' counsel, filed a brief in opposition to defendants' motion to dismiss with a history of reorganization and power of the DOR over GSP. Plaintiffs soon thereafter (9/20/73) served extensive first interrogatories on the defendants, requiring that they be answered or formally objected to by October 19, 1973.

Meanwhile, Commissioner MacDougall and Judge Alaimo coincidently considered mediation in the *Guthrie* dispute. MacDougall invited the Office of Community Relations Service of the U.S. Department of Justice to send a representative to act as mediator between GSP inmates and DOR representatives. Defendants' counsel Dorothy T. Beasley developed the legal strategy of mediation. The press channeled public pressures on the state to resolve matters in *Guthrie*. Beasley called Judge Jack M. Gordon in Baton Rouge, Louisiana, on September 12, 1973, about his use of mediation to resolve a dispute

over the Louisiana State Penitentiary. He referred her to mediator
Robert F. Greenwald of the Community Relations Service, U.S. De-
partment of Justice in Dallas, Texas. Greenwald seemed receptive to
Beasley's offer to mediate in the *Guthrie* suit, but required Judge
Alaimo's order to begin the proceedings.

Judge Alaimo ordered a preliminary conference of parties on October 10, 1973, to discuss the possibility of mediating some or all major
and minor issues in *Guthrie*. The parties apparently agreed to attempt
mediation, and on October 18, 1973, Judge Alaimo ordered mediation
under Robert F. Greenwald. Mediation was to begin on December 15,
1973, with written reports by parties submitted to the judge by January 4, 1974. One team included representative inmates and LDF attorneys, and the other consisted of DOR representatives (MacDougall or
Allen L. Ault, Caldwell or Hopper, and Samuel W. Austin) and counsel from the Georgia attorney general's office. The mediation was
divided into two phases. The first phase would consider matters
raised in the *Guthrie* amended complaint concerning racial discrimination against blacks. The second phase would take up other issues in
the amended complaint that concerned all GSP inmates, irrespective
of race. Representatives of all GSP inmates, white and black, would be
included in mediation on this second phase. Judge Alaimo further
directed that all *Guthrie* motions and interrogatories be set aside
pending the mediation. Thus, defendants did not have to formally
respond to the plaintiffs' interrogatories by October 19, 1973.

The plan for mediation was no sooner finalized when the U.S. Civil
Rights Commission held statewide hearings to assess prison conditions and the civil rights of inmates at all Georgia prisons. Meeting in
Atlanta, Georgia, on November 16 and 17, 1973, the commission
heard testimony from panels of legislators, private attorneys, medical
experts, the media, ministers, prior inmates, former correctional institution workers, present wardens in Georgia prisons, DOR Commissioner MacDougall, and numerous individuals. Commissioner Mac-
Dougall testified that the department could not find blacks to work in
Georgia prisons. Five former GSP inmates testified that assaults at
GSP were frequent because of snitching and homosexual rapes, particularly in the "official" gay dorms. They also testified that use of the
library was restricted, dorms and dining halls were segregated, inmates' attorney mail was censored, medical treatment was poor, and
black inmates were assigned the least desirable jobs. Legislators' tes-

timony noted the chronic underfunding of GSP and other Georgia prisons.

The stress of departmental reorganization, state politics, and *Guthrie* affected Commissioner MacDougall deeply. In May 1973 he suffered a heart attack and withdrew from *Guthrie* negotiations, sending his top aides, Dr. Allen L. Ault and Samuel W. Austin, in his place. With Lester Maddox's assumption of the governor's chair in 1973–74, there was talk of changing the state's position in *Guthrie*, of "getting tougher on convicts." MacDougall decided to leave with his appointing governor and officially resigned on December 31, 1973. He left for a position as associate dean in the College of Criminal Justice at the University of South Carolina, where he remains today.

Allen L. Ault was appointed DOR commissioner on January 1, 1974, and held the position until November 1976. As commissioner, Ault represented the department at the first negotiation sessions in January 1974. Assistant attorneys general David J. Bailey and David L. G. King joined Commissioner Ault in mediation sessions, replacing Dorothy Beasley. Bailey, born in Griffin, Georgia, in 1947, graduated Phi Beta Kappa from Duke University and was a classmate of LDF attorney Marilyn Holifield at Harvard Law School. Attorney General Bolton also brought in Don A. Langham, a labor negotiator at Lockheed Corporation and law graduate from Wayne State University, to help in mediation. Assistant Attorney General Richard L. Chambers, a 1948 University of Georgia law graduate, was designated the overseer of mediation and reported to Bolton.

The plan for mediation laid out by Greenwald emphasized that each team would first interpret its position on each of twenty-three issues presented in the amended complaint. Then, representatives of each team would come to the table to reach a mutually satisfactory solution. All matters agreed upon were to be set down in writing, signed by the principal parties and team members, and submitted to Judge Alaimo. If any issues were left unresolved, they would be tied together in a final settlement. The Phase I inmate team chairman was James Watson, and the Phase II inmate team co-chairmen were Joseph Beasley and Brannon Epps. Commissioner Ault was joined by Warden Hopper on the defendants' team.

The mediation teams agreed on one major point: the necessity of desegregating GSP. Judge Alaimo was elated with the result and issued an interim order on April 10, 1974, for the desegregation of all living and dining facilities at GSP. Commissioner Ault, Samuel Austin, and DOR staff developed the desegregation implementation plan and set a target date of April 15, 1974. The judge ordered a monitoring trio to inspect and report the progress of this desegregation effort. With the approval of prison officials, the inmates asked Eugene C. Tillman, a Brunswick, Georgia, minister and a member of the U.S. Civil Rights Commission, to be a member of the monitoring trio. With inmate representatives' approval, prison officials picked another member, John H. Thomas of Atlanta. Finally, Judge Alaimo appointed attorney Jack S. Hutto as special master and third member of the monitoring trio. Hutto was a Brunswick, Georgia, attorney and a LL.B. graduate of the John Marshall Law School in Atlanta, Georgia. Hutto was to stay on beyond the implementation of the desegregation plan to help set the stage for future mediation, settlement, and trial of all unresolved issues.

As directed by the court, GSP was desegregated on April 15. Warden Hopper reported that there were 55 percent black and 45 percent white inmates in all living areas. But desegregation was not effected without objection by the white inmates at GSP, who applied to intervene as plaintiffs in *Guthrie* for a stay of the desegregation order. Judge Alaimo put off responding until August 8, 1974, when he formally denied the white inmates' stay of order application. Alaimo was euphoric over the success of mediation and believed the parties were on verge of settling all issues.

But racial violence at GSP increased. After desegregation, incidents of physical abuse and verbal threats escalated. Mediation sessions increasingly became an escape valve for inmate complaints about conditions in the hypercharged atmosphere. The breakdown of communications in mediation stimulated inmates to seek other means of obtaining an audience with prison officials. On November 4, 1974, the inmates went on strike during work details and demanded to see Warden Hopper. Without provocation, GSP guards fired upon the inmates, killing one and wounding several others. Judge Alaimo held a hearing on November 13, 1974, to inquire into the incident pursuant to the plaintiffs' motion for a preliminary injunction and protective order. He issued no protective order, finding that the shooting "was not an intentional act of punishment of the inmates for any of their actions," but was the result of all participants contributing to a highly charged atmosphere.

Meanwhile, mediation had become frustrating and unsuccessful, despite the effort of the parties to negotiate a settlement on most issues. Defendants accused plaintiffs of injecting new and different issues into the negotiations. For example, plaintiffs spent much time raising the issues of hair length, the right to wear pendants and medallions, and privileges to use the prison store. Plaintiffs considered these minor, yet necessary, aspects of living conditions at GSP that related to the larger claims found in the amended complaint. Defendants felt these minor issues were outside the scope of mediation. Both Sanford Bishop and David Bailey agreed that more could be accomplished without Greenwald and mediation. On October 2, 1974, mediator Robert F. Greenwald wrote to Judge Alaimo recommending that mediation at GSP be terminated. Greenwald was troubled with the apparent failure of mediation in *Guthrie*, and had accepted a job with a mediation task force addressing Boston school desegregation.

However, Judge Alaimo was not willing to give up mediation. Under his instructions, Greenwald drew up plans for a last effort. Greenwald complained that there were too many attorneys and interested parties in attendance at the mediation sessions. These included six attorneys and parties from the State Board of Pardons and Parole, the Civil Rights Division of the U.S. Department of Justice, and the University of Georgia Institute of Government. Greenwald thought that the counsel for both parties was unable to adjust to the non-adversarial proceedings and unwilling to incorporate any agreements into a legally binding consent decree. He recommended that legal counsel be limited to two per side and positioned away from the mediation table so that communications would be directly exchanged by the parties. Outside observers would be admitted only upon mutual consent.

Mediation came to an end, in spite of Greenwald's suggestions, and the parties moved toward a trial of the issues. At a December 2, 1974, pre-trial conference, the parties told Judge Alaimo that it was impossible to negotiate a consent decree through mediation. Additionally, the parties consented to the appointment of a new special master to move them through pre-trial discovery.

On December 6, 1974, Judge Alaimo appointed Special Master Marvin L. Pipkin to conduct the next phase of the *Guthrie* litigation. An attorney from Saint Simons Island, Georgia, Pipkin was an A.B. and LL.B. graduate of Mercer University, and was admitted to the

Georgia Bar in 1961. Pipkin was instructed by Judge Alaimo to assist the parties in narrowing the issues for litigation, to conduct pre-trial discovery proceedings, to conduct the trial, and to make final findings of fact, reports, and recommendations to the court. Judge Alaimo identified eleven unresolved issues after meditation: (1) housing conditions, (2) inmate food and its distribution, (3) prison discipline and punishment, (4) visitation privileges, (5) inmate mail, (6) inmate literature, (7) staff training, qualifications, and discriminatory practices, (8) rehabilitative programs, (9) inmate grievances, (10) racial discrimination, and (11) inmate grooming. On December 23, 1974, Judge Alaimo included the issues raised by Muslim plaintiff inmates regarding their religious liberties. At this time, each party also submitted a proposed statement of issues for litigation.

Pipkin began conducting hearings in January 1975 to determine specific issues to be mediated and tried. Plaintiffs' counsel—Holifield, Walker, and Bishop—once again formally submitted interrogatories on the defendants. Almost all of 1975 and three-fourths of 1976 was spent in extensive pre-trial discovery procedures where both parties inquired into each others' case. Few issues were resolved beyond the filing of the amended complaint in 1973.

From December 1974 to July 1977, discovery by litigants included seven lengthy interrogatories, depositions of inmates and experts, and inspections of GSP files. Defendants' counsel, Bailey and King, fully expected to litigate the case all the way to the U.S. Supreme Court. They believed the plaintiffs' interrogatories were excessively long—some with 144 open-ended questions—and argued that plaintiffs were after information that was none of their business. Defendants' counsel sometimes answered with tongue in cheek:

Plaintiff's Q: What is the capacity of toilets at GSP?
Defendant's A: One inmate at a time.

Plaintiff's Q: How often are fire alarms tested at GSP?
Defendant's A: Once a day at noon and whenever inmates decide to wet their whistle and blow.

Plaintiffs' counsel did not consider the interrogatories sufficiently answered and obtained a court order to have all of them addressed again. During inspections of GSP files, some items were protected for reasons of prison security and order, but most were discoverable and photocopied at the defendants' expense. Some observers thought that the ordeal of discovery was simply a contest between the two Harvard Law School classmates, David Bailey and Marilyn Holifield. One observer commented, "You can't treat a case like this as adversarial . . . . Bailey and Holifield were fighting out who was the best Harvard lawyer."

Attorneys for the defendant-state made contact with other state attorney general offices, seeking information and strategies in litigating *Guthrie*. Members of the DOR and state attorney general's office attended a meeting with Alabama corrections and law officials on court-ordered prison reform in Alabama on February 19, 1976. They compared *Guthrie* with the Alabama prison case, *Pugh v. Locke*, 406 F. Supp. 318 (M.D. Ala. 1987), and discussed alternative strategies.

Meanwhile, GSP was bursting at the seams. As of October 12, 1975, nearly three thousand inmates were crowded into a facility originally designed for two thousand. Deputy Warden Ralph Kemp believed that GSP prisoners understood and accepted the overcrowded conditions, stating in 1975 that "[t]his is the calmest summer in years." It may have been the calm before the storm. One inmate commented, "All this training hasn't changed their attitude. . . . [GSP guards] pit the inmates against each other—we're fighting each other, there's less hassle for them."

From January through April 1976, prison officials worked to reduce the inmate population at GSP, emphasizing that overcrowding was the primary issue in the *Guthrie* litigation. Complicating this was the issue of punishment and protective custody. Disruptive inmates were housed separately, pending disciplinary hearings. These administrative segregation cells (M-building) were all double-bunked. Prison officials decided to convert these cells to single inmate occupancy and to transfer some of the inmates to the general population at GSP or to other prison institutions throughout the state. By August 1976, no inmates were assigned to M-building cells with another inmate.

Fact-finding hearings under Special Master Pipkin were lengthy and extensive, involving more than two hundred witnesses and one hundred exhibits over three phases from June 1976 to July 1977. Attorneys for plaintiffs included Sanford Bishop, Marilyn Holifield, and Lynn Walker. Attorneys for defendants included David Bailey,

James L. Mackey, Griffin Bell, Jr., and David L. G. King. Although King left to enter private practice in the summer of 1975, he stayed on for all hearings through the summer of 1977. Before the hearings, attorneys came close to settling the case, but defendants' counsel wouldn't agree to one item: ongoing monitoring by the court through to complete compliance.

The initial hearings from June 1976 through July 1976 included limited testimony by nine witnesses, including inmates, guards, and staff at GSP. Special Master Pipkin conducted nine days of hearings to determine if there had been improper use of force by staff against inmates and intimidation of inmates by staff to keep them from participating in the *Guthrie* litigation. Eleven transcribed volumes of testimony were taken. Pipkin did not make a finding of fact and report it to Judge Alaimo until November 26, 1976, after which the judge issued an order for the protection of inmates during the increasing violence at GSP pending the *Guthrie* trial. The parties would not enter into a consent decree relating to the monitoring, investigation, and standards on the improper use of force until August 1978.

Pipkin established a trial schedule from September 1976 through the summer of 1977 for litigation of *Guthrie* issues. Phase I of these hearings began in November 1976, after two months of postponement. During this time, Pipkin took ten full days of testimony that included only expert witnesses on general prison conditions, sanitation, food, medical services, and other GSP conditions and practices. Medical and penological experts offered opinions and recommendations based on their observations of sanitation and dietary, medical, and psychiatric services at GSP. Phase I resulted in ten transcribed volumes of testimony.

David C. Evans took control of GSP and the Georgia prison system as DOR commissioner on November 12, 1976. Dr. Allen Ault left to take charge of the newly created Mississippi Department of Corrections, embroiled in its own prison reform lawsuit (*Gates v. Collier*). Evans was only thirty-eight years old and had worked as budget director under Ault. He was chosen over practitioners in the field, such as James G. Rocketts (warden at Jackson Correctional Institution), because of his experience with state-level budgeting politics and his dedication to a new professionalism.

November 12, 1976, marked a day of violence at GSP. White inmates killed three black inmates, triggering a race riot that seriously

injured fifteen other white and black inmates. Alaimo responded
with a protective order issued on November 26, the first court order of
major importance since the desegregation order of April 10, 1974.
Alaimo enjoined the defendants from failing to protect inmates from
attack by other inmates, and required GSP to post correctional officers
on every floor of every housing unit and at the entrance to dormitories
on a twenty-four-hour basis.

Alaimo's November 26 protective order also enjoined the defendants from "employing unwarranted or unnecessary use of force." In
this respect, Alaimo responded to a November 9 incident at GSP in
which three correctional officers used excessive force to subdue an
inmate who refused to submit to a strip search. The officers broke the
inmate's leg. The incident appeared to have sparked the riot three
days later. DOR staff reviewed the incident and agreed that the force
was excessive. The three officers were dismissed on November 22.
(Eighteen months later, the State Merit System reinstated them with
back pay.)

The November 26 protective order also required the defendants to
allow plaintiffs' counsel reasonable access to GSP to interview their
clients and potential witnesses for litigation. Defendants were also
required to post notice of the protective order and to make all GSP
personnel and inmates aware of its contents.

DOR Commissioner Evans responded quickly to the violence at
GSP by requesting and receiving an emergency requisition of forty-
eight additional correctional officers. At first, plaintiffs' counsel suggested that 42 percent, then 100 percent of the new positions be filled
with blacks. They reasoned that hiring more black guards at GSP
would indicate that the defendants were sincere in their effort to
mitigate issues raised in the *Guthrie* complaint. Defendants argued
that affirmative action in hiring DOR employees was part of a statewide program that went beyond the scope of *Guthrie* and GSP. Of
course, plaintiffs did not formally incorporate this new issue into
Guthrie, but these and other suggestions to the court in effect expanded the lawsuit to include new issues, making quick resolution of
Guthrie impossible.

At this time (1976) more than four years had passed since the
original *in forma pauperis* complaint had been filed, yet the parties
were still unable to agree on even the scope of the litigation and the
limits of the issues involved. Soon, however, the defendants compromised, and by January 1977, Commissioner Evans announced that

half of the forty-eight new positions at GSP had been filled with black correctional officers. On January 1, 1977, Governor George Busbee announced that the new budget for fiscal year 1978 included $10.8 million for construction of new facilities to relieve prison overcrowding at GSP. On February 2, 1977, Special Master Pipkin ordered single inmate occupancy in GSP administrative segregation.

The violence at GSP continued. On May 30, 1977, white inmates roaming the corridors of GSP seriously injured several black inmates with spears made of metal scraps and broomsticks. In a meeting on October 12, 1977, the board of DOR expressed extreme concern with the increasing racial violence at GSP. The Georgia State Board of Corrections and Offender Rehabilitation then formed an investigatory committee on prison conditions and took testimony from ex-inmates, interested citizens, ministers, and ACLU representatives on GSP racial violence.

This concern spread. On December 2, plaintiffs' counsel Lynn Walker spoke to a lunch audience in Atlanta and described racial atrocities and violence at GSP. On December 12, more than two hundred people participated in a demonstration in Atlanta to protest the "racist attacks in Reidsville."

Phase II hearings did not begin until March 1977 and ran through July 1977. The hearings dealt with virtually every aspect of *Guthrie*. Particular attention was focused on medical care and allegations of racial discrimination in prison discipline at GSP. The hearings included testimony from nearly 180 witnesses, mostly inmates and defendants, as well as experts on almost every aspect of inmate life at GSP. Over one hundred exhibits were introduced.

During the initial hearings in June 1976, inmate Albert Henderson testified about misconduct by plaintiffs' counsel, the attorneys from the Legal Defense Fund of the NAACP. He testified that inmates were encouraged by plaintiffs' counsel to stir up violence at the prison for pre-trial publicity and to perjure themselves at the hearings with tales of inmate beatings and GSP atrocities. Georgia Attorney General Arthur Bolton called for an investigation by the U.S. district attorney into possible professional misconduct by plaintiffs' counsel. Henderson later confessed on August 16, 1977, that he was lying in the hope of a favorable parole decision. His testimony was stricken from the record by Special Master Pipkin, and all charges of professional misconduct were dropped.

For approximately twelve months following the hearings conducted by Special Master Pipkin, the parties developed "proposed findings of facts and conclusions of law." While both parties continued negotiations toward a consent decree, Special Master Pipkin ordered them to summarize the sixty-nine volumes of transcribed testimony and more than one hundred exhibits and to submit their findings by July 30, 1978. Pipkin was aware of the stalemate in negotiations toward a consent decree and thought that careful reflection on the facts and law would lead to some agreement. The defendants submitted their proposed findings and conclusions on July 27, 1978. The plaintiffs did not submit theirs until May 18, 1979. Even after more than twelve months of research and reflections on the extensive record of the case, the parties were still in considerable disagreement over the scope and appropriate remedies for the issues in *Guthrie*. This delay exacerbated two problems: the turnover of counsel and, more importantly, the increasing unrest in the inmate population.

In early 1978, fire struck the prison chapel. Arson was suspected, and investigators determined that the fire may have originated with, or was initiated in retaliation against, members of the Inmate Unity Committee, a group of politically active inmates seeking prison union status. Five key group members were placed in administrative segregation pending an internal investigation and possible criminal charges. Plaintiffs' counsel in *Guthrie* represented the five and filed a writ of habeas corpus in the Federal District Court for the Northern District of Georgia. They asked the court to enjoin defendants from confining the five inmates in administrative segregation. The defendants argued that there were obvious safety and security reasons for confinement, and moved to transfer the case to the U.S. District Court for the Southern District of Georgia for proper venue. After the case was transferred, Judge Edenfield, assigned to the case, ruled in favor of the defendants and dismissed the writ of habeas corpus.

In March 1978, black inmates retaliated for previous attacks by white inmates. The fighting lasted an entire night and resulted in the death of one black inmate and injuries to sixteen other white and black inmates. Black inmates again retaliated on June 24 for the inmate death in March by attacking white inmates at the inmates' movie theater and injuring several. On July 1, a group of white inmates seeking revenge attacked a group of black inmates returning from breakfast. One black inmate was killed.

Special Master Pipkin, believing that the violence would get worse, urged the judge to re-segregate GSP to avoid further bloodshed. In an April 7, 1978, speech, Governor Busbee blamed the court-ordered integration for increased prison violence at GSP and commented, "To be very candid, I don't think it's humanly possible to prevent murder in prisons, totally. . . . I think it's racially inspired." Counsel for plaintiffs and defendants objected, because both considered such a step regressive. Also, they feared even more violence. After the tremendous increase in violence the following June and July, Judge Alaimo on July 3, 1978, ordered the temporary separation of inmates by race. According to Alaimo's order, each dormitory consisted of either white or black inmates arranged in a checkerboard pattern of black dorm, white dorm. Judge Alaimo further ordered a reduction in inmate population and specified a change of six hundred inmates. GSP and DOR officials had already initiated a plan to reduce GSP inmate population, but were ordered to step up the operation. An inmate advocacy group, the Human Rights for Prisoners Committee, asked Judge Alaimo to abandon his order for the checkerboard pattern, claiming that the "mixing of prisoners during mass movements will heighten anxieties and may lead to attacks." On July 15, 1978, about three hundred inmates were transferred from GSP to other Georgia facilities.

The violence at GSP was not mitigated by the re-segregation order. Instead, the movement of inmates out of GSP and the checkerboard arrangement seemed to heighten racial tensions. On July 23, 1978, entire dorms of inmates attacked other dorms. The riot was apparently prompted by one the day before by black inmates at the Pontiac, Illinois, prison in which three Illinois guards were killed and six others injured. At GSP, black inmates from two dorms attacked white inmates and correctional officers of both races. In the end, two white inmates and one white officer were dead. Two other white officers were taken hostage by inmates but survived, although one was critically injured with a serious stab wound.

In response, GSP administrators ordered an immediate and total lock down. For several weeks, inmates' movements were almost totally restricted, and inside and outside work details were almost completely cut. Only a few trustee inmates were allowed to move around. DOR administrators assigned correctional officers with experience in riot control to GSP. Even under lock down, on August 16, white inmates managed a revenge attack on black inmates, killing one and

injuring three others. In a crackdown by DOR investigators, eight
prison workers were forced to resign on September 15 after it was
discovered that they had sold contraband and allowed some inmates
to keep weapons.

The July 23, 1978, killing of correctional officer Dan Harrison by an
inmate led by a group of homosexual inmates motivated the Georgia
legislature and governor in a way the *Guthrie* lawsuit had not. Immediately upon hearing of the tragedy, Governor George Busbee called a
meeting with his friend Paul C. Rosser, president of Justice Systems,
Inc., a prison construction company, DOR Commissioner Evans, and
others. Busbee wanted immediate solutions at GSP and incredulously
asked, "How can this happen at a maximum security prison?" Rosser
and Evans pointed out that GSP was not designed as a maximum
security prison, but was modeled after federal facilities for youthful
offenders. Only a fence kept inmates from breaking out. Rosser presented the governor with slides showing the prison's outdated plumbing, small visiting space, and overcrowded dormitories fronting on a
narrow central corridor. The group considered several alternatives:
build a new prison, renovate GSP, or ignore maximum security problems since the *Guthrie* lawsuit didn't require these changes anyway.
To ignore security problems and go to total lock down wasn't feasible,
but the cost of building a new 2,000-bed facility was prohibitive in the
recessed Georgia economy. The estimated cost of such a facility in
1978 was about $120,000,000, or $60,000 per bed. The group decided
to renovate GSP.

Governor Busbee's emergency fund and matching funds from the
Law Enforcement Assistance Administration provided $1.2 million
for the first short-term security plan, Project 90, so-called because the
changes were to be made within ninety days. The funds were used to
install secure officer stations, electric locks, sallyport gates for inmate passage, and intercommunication systems.

A long-term security plan, Project 360, with a fiscal year 1979
budget appropriation of $6.8 million, included a complete renovation
of GSP that started in the fall of 1978. The plan would include (1) 1,850
single cells of 80 square feet each, with individual plumbing and air
vents, (2) new guard towers erected around the premises for better
visibility, (3) visitation and dining rooms for each living unit of 26 to
28 cells, (4) monitoring and control stations with maximum visibility
of four living units (104 to 112 cells on two levels), (5) a completely
enclosed two-level walkway creating a perimeter around the original

buildings and forming twelve individual exercise areas between dormitories, and (6) total renovation of administrative segregation (isolation) in a separate building. Adjoining the original building on the east were new constructions: a court hearing room, library, and reception rooms. Replacing the old Building 2, which was located across the highway from the main building, was a new minimum security facility, the Richard H. "Dicky" Rogers Correctional Institution.[1] It was designed to house approximately four hundred minimum security inmates who would raise and prepare food for GSP use.

From 1978 through 1985, Paul Rosser's prison construction company, Justice Systems, Inc., received $55,900,000 for the renovation of 1,850 cells at GSP and the facilities for four hundred inmates at the new Rogers Correctional Institution. Although the work took much longer than the originally estimated 360 days, Rosser asserted that the state saved more than 50 percent over the cost of new construction (Rosser, in Southern Conference on Corrections, 1986). Participants in projects 90 and 360 quickly point out that the *Guthrie* lawsuit itself did not prompt the decision to renovate GSP, although it was certainly related. The renovation was never part of the pleadings, stipulations, or consent decrees in the case. However, Judge Alaimo and others in the *Guthrie* case saw it as a watershed for inmates' constitutional rights in areas of prison conditions and practices.

To complete the litigation in *Guthrie*, Special Master Pipkin submitted a series of reports to Judge Alaimo summarizing facts, reporting progress on a consent decree, and recommending further action by the court. Judge Alaimo's first endorsement of these reports came on July 3, 1977, and December 30, 1977. Many of the reports formed the basis for ongoing and contemporaneous negotiation by the parties toward a consent decree. By the time Pipkin had filed reports on all instructed areas, the parties had reached agreement for the consent decree on all issues presented. On October 8, 1979, Pipkin filed his final report on the two issues not yet settled by negotiations between parties, racial discrimination in the imposition of inmate discipline, and the adequacy of medical services for inmates.

Pipkin concluded that there was no evidence that defendants imposed inmate discipline in a racially discriminatory manner. Pipkin stated in his final report:

> [T]he studies conducted by either [plaintiffs' or defendants'] expert clearly show that race as a factor is not determinative in the degree of

severity of punishment throughout the period studied. . . . [T]he Plaintiffs have failed to show racial bias or discrimination of Blacks in the imposition or severity of punishment [for the period 1973 through 1975].

However, Pipkin determined that GSP medical facilities were wholly inadequate and understaffed, and that transporting inmates with serious injuries to Augusta, Georgia, for treatment was not feasible. The medical staff was overworked and underqualified, and the prison hospital was unsanitary. The defendants failed to meet standards clearly established by various federal district courts, the Fifth and Sixth Circuit Court of Appeals, and the U.S. Supreme Court.

The defendant-state formally objected to Pipkin's finding on the medical treatment at GSP. Defendants' counsel argued that these conditions, although poor, did not violate the Eighth Amendment prohibition of cruel and unusual punishment. Yet the defendants eventually agreed with the recommendations Pipkin made to Judge Alaimo: that the court monitor personnel recruitment for new staff at GSP, completion of the Augusta Medical and Correctional Facility, building of the Metro Atlanta Community Correctional Institution, and plans to improve medical procedures and practices at GSP. Pipkin was convinced that defendants were headed toward compliance, commenting:

> Provided that the plans for the completion of the Augusta and Atlanta facilities are carried out in a timely manner, there should be no need for further medical relief to inmates at the Georgia State Prison. . . . Once implemented, they would resolve the two most serious problems in health care of inmates, specifically: adequate hospital facilities and staff personnel.

Pipkin also recommended that Judge Alaimo closely monitor the resolution of *Guthrie* by retaining jurisdiction, overseeing consent decrees, and maintaining the already appointed special monitor. Pipkin was confident that *Guthrie* was over with the filing of this final report. Judge Alaimo endorsed these reports in their entirety.

4

Designing Remedies in *Guthrie*

The Law of Institutional Remedies

With increasing judicial involvement in the administration of prison reform, the traditional remedies at law have become inappropriate. Monetary damages to individual plaintiffs have had little effect on improving prison conditions. Judges have turned instead to remedial decrees at a structural, institution-wide level to change conditions and practices. A wide range of remedies is provided for by 42 U.S.C. 1983; once a federal civil rights violation is established, the violator is liable "in an action at law, suit in equity, or other proper proceeding for redress." Liability at law may result in nominal, compensatory, or punitive monetary damages, while liability in equity may result in declaratory or injunctive relief. The Constitution recognizes this equity jurisdiction in Article III and permits use of these remedies. Most prison institutional reform litigation cases receive equitable relief with broad remedial decrees to effect institution-wide reforms.

Holt v. Sarver, 309 F. Supp. 362 (E.D. Ark. 1970), was one of the first cases where federal courts issued structural, institution-wide remedial decrees for equitable relief of prison conditions. The court issued about forty decrees, affecting almost every phase of prison operations. Remedial decrees even ordered the building of a new maximum security prison in Arkansas, but this was reversed on appeal.

Following the Supreme Court's lead in *Swann v. Charlotte-Mecklenburg Board of Education*, 402 U.S. 1, at 15 (1971), federal district courts have constructed broad and flexible remedial decrees to redress institution-wide problems. Remedial decrees by courts have ordered changes in prison sanitation, food preparation, temperature control, fire control, industries, and ventilation. They have also mandated inmate classification, safety and security measures, disciplinary

procedures, racial discrimination, grievance procedures, overcrowding restrictions, religious freedoms, law library access, visitation
privileges, educational programs, segregation, rehabilitation, exercise privileges, and medical, dental, and mental health programs.

Judges typically urge out-of-court settlement by consent decrees to
avoid the burdensome duties associated with decree formulation, implementation, and enforcement. Institutional reform litigation, like
all federal class actions, can be settled only by entry of court approval
under F.R.Civ.P. Rule 23 (e). To approve a consent decree, then, a
court must have jurisdiction and independently evaluate the terms of
the consent decree. Federal courts have subject matter jurisdiction if
the case raises any non-frivolous federal question on the face of the
complaint and if it involves a representative class of plaintiffs, *Mt.
Health City Board of Education v. Doyle*, 429 U.S. 274, pp. 278–79,
(1977). The court must also independently assess that the settlement
is fair, reasonable, consistent with actual law, and in the best interests
of those affected, *Costello v. Wainwright*, 489 F. Supp. 1100 (M.D.
Fla. 1980), and *Washington v. Keller*, 479 F. Supp. 569 (D. Md. 1979).
A court evaluates the settlement as a whole, rather than by each provision, for a totality of conditions. This is designed to ensure adequate
representation to protect absent class members' interests (Boston, in
Bronstein, 1981). However, consent decree approval is rarely the end
of the prison case. Courts usually must enforce the decree with the
mechanisms discussed above.

Remedy Phase: 1977–85

The remedy phase follows the liability phase in most institutional
reform litigation (Cooper, 1988). All remedial decrees, including
judicial orders and consent decrees, are formulated by a process of
negotiation, stipulation, and formal court review and order, and are
usually accompanied by a parallel appeals process. At this remedy-
crafting stage of a prison reform lawsuit, the parties' attorneys typically confer with one another and with the judge to develop and
formally decide on a core remedy, such as the use of contempt citations or retaining jurisdiction.

For example, in the Mississippi prison case of *Gates v. Collier*, 349
F. Supp. 881 (N.D. Miss. 1972), Judge Keady issued a comprehensive
injunctive order only eight months after the case was initiated, along

with findings of fact and conclusions of law. The injunction granted immediate and long-term relief. Specific points included inmate mail, inmate segregation, medical treatment, and inmate classification, as well as prison overcrowding, increased use of alternatives to incarceration, and construction of new housing. The defendant-state appealed the case immediately to the Fifth Circuit Court of Appeals, where it was eventually affirmed in 1974 (Cooke and Panko, 1986). The Alabama prison case in *Pugh v. Locke*, 406 F. Supp. 318 (M.D. Al. 1976), was similar. In that case, Judge Johnson issued a comprehensive injunction after rendering a finding of fact in a trial proceeding (Yarbrough, 1981).

Guthrie is unique because its long and extended negotiation toward final consent decrees lasted from the early consent decree negotiation in 1977 to the final permanent injunction issued June 26, 1985. The uniquely long duration of the remedy phase in *Guthrie* may be due to three factors: (1) the liability phase never went to full, formal trial litigation, (2) Judge Alaimo did not issue litigated remedies, but pushed consent decrees already negotiated by the parties, and (3) no appeals were made to change the scope or nature of consent decrees or federal court intervention. These factors are largely attributed to a commitment made to Judge Alaimo by Georgia Governor George D. Busbee and continued by Governor Joe Frank Harris. This commitment consisted of an end to federal court intervention, coupled with the development of a model penal system in Georgia. Consequently, these governors directed the attorneys general and DOR officials to negotiate, rather than litigate, the issues in *Guthrie*. Judge Alaimo retained jurisdiction throughout the case and, after substantial implementation, issued court approval of these negotiated consent decrees with a final injunctive order. Because of the dynamic and lengthy nature of remedy formulation, the remedies in this phase of *Guthrie* appear to creep along in ever-enlarging increments until the final injunctive order in 1985.

DOR Commissioner David Evans had no sooner taken office in 1976 than *Guthrie* grabbed all his time and attention. For the next few years, he to tried to quell the violence at GSP, to litigate before Special Master Pipkin, to direct the defendants' position in negotiation, and to lobby the state governor and legislature for funds. Important non-procedural orders and consent decrees before Evans took office were relatively few, designed only to push GSP until a finding of facts was completed. These included an order on April 10, 1974, to complete racial integration at GSP and a November 26, 1976, order for the protection and safety of inmates at GSP during litigation before Special Master Pipkin.

Until 1977, the GSP warden and his staff coordinated the defendant-state's position in *Guthrie* negotiations with the Georgia attorney general's office, while DOR central office staff responded with information and advice. In January 1977, Commissioner Evans made the central office the focal point for the defendant-state's position, with DOR Assistant Commissioner Samuel W. Austin working full-time on *Guthrie*. Evans and Austin realized that a statewide effort was necessary to resolve the problems at GSP. For example, it was obvious to them that a final settlement on overcrowding would require moving inmates from GSP to other state prisons. Furthermore, *Guthrie* was influencing other state prisons where inmates were starting to litigate for similar changes in prison conditions and practices.

The parties had come closer to an agreement to agree. A revised working draft of a stipulation to negotiate toward consent decrees had circulated during 1977–78. This negotiation took place simultaneously with litigation before Special Master Pipkin during Phase I and II hearings in 1976 and 1977. The proposed stipulation included sections addressing overcrowding, racial discrimination, improper use of force, food and conditions of preparation, imposition of discipline, conditions and use of administrative segregation, the rights of Muslim inmates, classification procedures, housing orderly and hospital job assignments, fire prevention and control, and inmate grievance procedures. Negotiators included LDF attorneys Ralston, Holifield, and Walker, as well as assistant attorneys general King and Bailey. James L. Mackay, a young assistant attorney general with a law degree from the University of Texas, also worked briefly as defendants' counsel in 1977–78. Although David King had left the Georgia attorney general's office in the summer of 1975, he continued to work on the *Guthrie* hearings and negotiations through 1977. The parties came close to settling the case before the 1976–77 hearings, but their oral agreements were never satisfactorily written down. Plaintiffs' counsel found important omissions in the proposed consent decrees drafted by defendants' counsel and refused to sign, thus threatening further litigation. The defendants were opposed to ongoing monitoring by the federal court and refused to compromise with plaintiffs' counsel on that point. Only marginal agreement could be reached on whether or not the consent decree met constitutional standards.

The spring and summer of 1978 marked great changes in the personnel and remedy of the *Guthrie* dispute. LDF attorneys Ralston, Holifield, and Walker moved out of the case in 1978 after litigation before Special Master Pipkin was completed. Before leaving, plaintiffs' counsel Lynn Walker asked Robert W. Cullen, an attorney with the Augusta legal services office, to give a speech to the Georgia Medical Association about prison reform. Cullen was only twenty-nine years old and a recent member of the Georgia Bar. However, he had distinguished himself in a 1977 case on the institutional reform of the Richmond County (Georgia) Jail. Cullen litigated this 1977 case before Judge Alaimo, who thus came to know and respect him. From these contacts with plaintiffs' counsel and Judge Alaimo, Cullen was informally selected to work as plaintiffs' counsel to negotiate and resolve the five-year-old case. In March 1978, Judge Alaimo asked him to work as plaintiffs' counsel in *Guthrie* and Cullen accepted; however, no formal notice of appearance was recorded by the court until June 1978. The Legal Defense Fund remained active in the case, assigning New York attorney Steven L. Winter to the case from 1978 to 1985 as co-counsel with Cullen, who essentially took over the plaintiff-inmates' case from 1978 through 1986.

The defendants' counsel also changed in June 1978. Georgia Attorney General Arthur K. Bolton assigned assistant attorneys general John C. Walden and Harrison Kohler to negotiate and settle the case. Walden, a native of Augusta, graduated with an A.B. and LL.B. from Mercer University and was admitted to the Georgia Bar in 1965. He began as an assistant attorney general on January 1, 1969, and was promoted to head of the criminal division in July 1976. Kohler began work with the criminal division of the Georgia attorney general's office upon graduation from Emory University Law School in 1975.

These personnel changes marked an abrupt change of style in the *Guthrie* litigation. Until this time, counsel for plaintiffs and defendants were fierce adversaries in a win-or-lose battle. Certain assistant attorneys general fully expected to appeal the case all the way to the Supreme Court. However, Governor Busbee and Attorney General Bolton were approached by Judge Alaimo at this time to settle *Guthrie* and "do what's right" by "cleaning up" GSP. Busbee and Bolton accepted this position and funded the necessary changes, despite the state's deep economic recession at the time. More importantly, this position was accepted by their successors, Governor Joe Frank Harris and Attorney General Michael J. Bowers.

After relocating the negotiation authority in *Guthrie* with the DOR central office, DOR Commissioner Evans began sifting through the proposed stipulations to the case's first consent decree. He believed only a miracle could transform the fragmented and vague goals of both sides into a comprehensive consent decree to which all parties could agree. Piecemeal agreements and stipulations were the most he could hope for. Negotiations proceeded in that fashion.

The first agreement produced was a consent decree issued on July 19, 1978. This decree pertained to access to a law library and legal assistance at GSP. In their amended complaint, inmates alleged that they were denied access to legal counsel because GSP visitation facilities were not conducive to confidential attorney-client conversation. However, counsel for the defendants and plaintiffs did not design this consent decree in response to these allegations. Rather, the consent decree was based on the parties' adherence to a recent U.S. Supreme Court ruling, *Bounds v. Smith*, 430 U.S. 817 (1977), where the Court held that a state prison must provide inmates adequate access to legal assistance, either with a good law library or readily available attorneys. The defendants were not nearly as concerned with the effect of *Bounds* on GSP as they were with its impact on another class action lawsuit, *Hardwick v. Ault*, by inmates in administrative segregation at the Georgia Diagnostic and Classification Center in Jackson, Georgia. Administrative segregation inmates at the Jackson facility also needed access to a law library, but could not mingle with the general population in a library and at the same time be isolated from other inmates. Plaintiffs' counsel was more concerned with facilitating GSP inmate needs for legal assistance as soon as possible and considered *Bounds* a mandate to the state.

The July 19, 1978, consent decree provided for greater access to legal counsel and the creation of a law library. If not allowed access to the law library, an administrative segregation inmate could have adequate legal assistance through legal counsel. Lawyers and legal interns were provided through the Prisoner Legal Counseling Project of the University of Georgia School of Law. This consent decree went beyond the bounds of GSP, however, as it had a statewide effect. Consequently, the PLCP attorneys were given access to virtually all state and county correctional institutions in Georgia.

The parties reached agreement on their most comprehensive decree, which was approved by Judge Alaimo on August 4, 1978. This occurred during submission of the findings of fact and conclusions of law based on the hearings before Special Master Pipkin in 1976 and 1977 (see chapter 3). The decree included and went beyond every major issue raised by the *Guthrie* 1974 amended complaint. It included stipulations related to overcrowding; racial discrimination against inmates and GSP employees; guidelines on the improper use of force; food and food preparation; disciplinary proceedings; administrative segregation conditions and procedures; mail and visitation privileges and procedures; guidelines on inmate property, books, and publications; inmate relations with attorneys; religious liberties of Muslim inmates; procedures for inmate classification; assignment of coveted housing orderly and hospital jobs; fire prevention and control; and inmate grievance procedures. Each section of the consent decree incorporated numerous DOR and GSP rules and regulations.

Essentially, the consent decree was a revision of the proposed stipulation presented to DOR Commissioner Evans when he assumed departmental leadership in 1976. During the negotiations the scope and detail of each section were expanded, and sections on inmate mail, visitation privileges, attorney-client relations, books and publications, and distribution of the order were attached. The consent decree required defendants to begin immediate implementation of all stipulations and set up a schedule for inspection and approval by Judge Alaimo: (1) within 30 days re-screen all inmates assigned to house orderly and hospital jobs; establish a committee to review inmate grievances of verbal and physical abuse; allow Muslim inmates out of administrative segregation if they wish (held since the June 22, 1974, incident over racial desegregation), (2) within 60 days re-evaluate all administrative segregation inmates held over six months, documenting reasons for any continued assignment, and (3) within 180 days develop detailed crowd (riot) control procedures.

Tensions between inmates and inmate-guards at GSP had not subsided during this quiet negotiation. A Tattnall County grand jury investigation in the spring of 1978 reported that federal court-ordered integration at GSP had contributed to repeated bloody clashes between white and black inmates. The grand jury appealed to Judge Alaimo to allow GSP officials to "make assignments of the inmate population in such a manner as to remove the explosive racial situation now present" and to reduce inmate population by at least 700. Reporting an

inmate count near 2,600 in 1978, GSP Warden Hopper reacted by
abolishing the Inmate Unity Committee, which was formally created
to air inmate grievances but was now the focus of a struggle between
black and white inmates.

Warden Hopper was apparently experiencing problems with GSP
guards and DOR administrators. Guards talked of unionizing and held
a meeting at the river at the back of GSP grounds. It was reputed that
DOR Deputy Commissioner E. B. Caldwell, former GSP warden, was
trying to control GSP activities. The power struggle between Hopper
and Caldwell allowed dissatisfied GSP personnel to go from one to the
other for favorable treatment. This frustrating situation prompted Warden Hopper to make a remark to the press that was later taken as a
challenge by Warden Lanson Newsome: "It doesn't matter who is the
warden of Georgia State Prison—Jesus Christ Himself couldn't solve
the problems without adequate financial support in combination with
good management" (*The Atlanta Constitution,* 4/15/80).

Warden Hopper was relieved of his position at GSP, and a new warden, Charles Balkcom, was appointed on August 15, 1978. Balkcom
had been raised at GSP; his father, Robert, was the GSP warden from
1948 to 1965, and Charles served as a guard at GSP from 1959 to 1970.
Balkcom had demonstrated a conservative and disciplined approach
as warden of the Georgia Industrial Institute at Alto in 1970. He also
built the Montgomery, Georgia, Correctional Institution and served as
its first warden in 1971. At various correctional institutions in Georgia,
Balkcom also initiated educational, literacy, and treatment programs.

Balkcom came to GSP shortly after the notorious July 23, 1978, riot
in which one guard and two inmates were murdered. The prison was
overcrowded and understaffed. The guards had been working thirty-
eight straight days. Inmates were writing to the ACLU about graft and
corruption among GSP staff. In response, the governor ordered an
investigation by the Georgia Bureau of Investigation (GBI). This investigation uncovered corruption at GSP and resulted in the firing of
twenty-three guards accused of providing drugs, weapons, and sex to
inmates for bribes. The day after Balkcom's appointment as warden, a
group of white inmates attacked a group of black inmates in retaliation for the July 23 incident. One black inmate was murdered and
three others injured. Morale at GSP was at its lowest point, and any
attempts to implement *Guthrie* consent decrees were abandoned in
what seemed a futile effort to impose order on a violent summer.

Warden Balkcom placed gun stations made of sandbags and machine guns in the hallways at GSP. The stations truly symbolized the warlike conditions at GSP, but they eased the burden on personnel. Instead of using fifteen guards to escort a dormful of inmates to the dining hall, a handful of guards at gun stations could effectively control the inmates. Guards could now take days off. Judge Alaimo provided further relief by extending "until further notice" the checkerboard dorm segregation originally ordered on July 3, 1978.

Negotiations continued in the meantime, producing another major consent decree adopted by the court on December 1, 1978. These stipulations covered areas not included in the more comprehensive 8/4/78 consent decree, such as vocational, academic, and rehabilitation programs; general library services; pork-free diets; continued overcrowding; security renovations; personal property of inmates; hiring of personnel; and plaintiff-inmates' response to this and the 8/4/78 consent decrees. The 12/1/78 consent decree also required defendants to complete certain tasks within specified deadlines: (1) over the following 180 days provide a pork-free diet for a trial period of 180 days to see if inmate demand warranted a permanent pork-free menu, (2) within one month reduce overcrowding in the main complex of GSP to 1,850 inmates and install an intercom system between guard stations and central control (defendants also stipulated Project 90 had been completed by 12/1/78), (3) within six months submit a detailed plan for provision of vocational, academic, and rehabilitative programs for GSP inmates, to be implemented within twelve months (6/1/80) if the plan is approved by the court and plaintiffs' counsel, and (4) within two years reduce prison population to 1,750 inmates in the main complex of GSP by 1/1/81. General library services provided for the GSP inmates were vastly increased by the 12/1/78 consent decree, above and beyond the requirements already imposed by the 8/4/78 consent decree for a law library. Required were a minimum of ten thousand non-legal books (fiction and non-fiction), subscriptions to at least four different daily newspapers, and subscriptions to various news magazines. Even more important to plaintiff-inmates was the increased service and access to library materials. GSP administrators agreed to expand library hours, give priority access to inmates on outside work details, provide book cart service to inmates in isolation, and secure at least 15 percent of library holdings in Afro-American culture and history. A librarian was also provided for typing inmate legal documents.

Through the next twelve months, DOR officials gave their full attention to GSP, making 1979 a critical year in the resolution of *Guthrie* issues. Judge Alaimo set events in motion with an order on December 12, 1978, in which he outlined the big changes he envisioned at GSP for 1979. Although extending the checkerboard dormitory segregation of races, the order directed DOR and GSP officials to devise an integration plan by January 15, 1979, and to integrate the prison in a short and complete move, rather than the piecemeal efforts previously attempted. The plan was to provide for no fewer than 45 percent white inmates and no more than 55 percent black inmates in each integrated dormitory. Integration was to be in effect by March 1, 1979. Alaimo went further in the 12/12/78 order to officially recognize the long-range redevelopment plans of DOR in Project 360. He included certain of these already in-place changes in his order for integration: adequate security staffing and devices, the move to single inmate occupancy from open dormitories, and a long-term security plan. Though never mandated by Judge Alaimo, these changes in the physical structure of GSP appeared to dramatically change the life and conditions of the prison.

As the major issues of the *Guthrie* lawsuit were resolved by the consent decrees of 1978, the attention of parties in the case focused on the implementation of these decrees. However, the formulation of important remedies did not cease, and the comprehensive consent decrees of 1978 were under constant revision. New remedies from 1978 through 1985 reflected the many changes at GSP, changes in its physical plant (due to Project 360), inmate composition, professionalization of GSP staff, new parties to the litigation, and the influence of the special monitor. Important non-procedural orders and consent decrees from 1978 to 1985 are too numerous to itemize. No less than sixty-one orders and consent decrees were handed down to resolve GSP problems in three major areas: (1) physical health and safety of GSP inmates, (2) due process of law and the equal protection of the laws in the fair treatment of GSP inmates and in GSP employment practices, and (3) medical services, vocational and educational programs, and rehabilitative incentive plans for GSP inmates. Individual summaries of these orders and consent decrees are placed in chronological order in Appendix B.

5

Implementing Rights in *Guthrie*

The Law of Implementation

Constructing a remedial decree is only the beginning of prison reform litigation. In ordinary litigation, entry of a judgment marks the end of the court's involvement in the case. But in institutional reform litigation, a court must devise an implementation scheme with a remedial decree and take a more active part in assuring compliance. Courts typically appoint others to help them gather facts during the remedy-crafting and implementation periods. These appointments include special masters and monitors, receivers, ombudsmen, human rights committees, and expert panels.

Special masters are most commonly used. Federal district courts appoint masters under F.R.Civ.P. 53 by a letter of reference, which assigns a special master to a specific case with enumerated powers. Masters may be appointed to help in crafting a remedial decree, but are more often used to oversee implementation. The broad power given masters often results in highly intrusive and daily involvement in prison administration. Courts have taken steps to limit the master's authority (e.g., requiring notices throughout a jail specifying the exact limits of the master's powers and affirming the authority of the prison administration, as in *Jones v. Wittenberg*, 73 F.R.D. 82, at 86 [N.D. Ohio 1976]). Yet the role of the master often expands to include fact-finding, mediation, monitoring, enforcement, management, and planning (Brakel, 1986A; Levine, 1984; Liles, 1987; Nathan, 1979).

Some appointed officers (special masters) are simply referred to by a court as monitors. A monitor typically has the more limited task of overseeing implementation and reporting to the court. Monitors were used in *Gates v. Collier*, 349 F. Supp. 881 (N.D. Miss. 1972) after administrative noncompliance. In these instances, monitors reviewed prison operations, records, and administration and gave direct reports to the court for day-to-day scrutiny.

Receivers were traditionally appointed in bankruptcy proceedings, but are now used by courts to protect civil rights in institutional reform litigation (Comment, 1976; Eisenberg and Yeazell, 1980). The powers given a master are often just short of the actual managerial control given to a receiver. In *Newman v. Alabama,* 466 F. Supp. 628 (M.D. Ala. 1979), the court decided that the Alabama Board of Corrections was not serious about compliance and placed its prisons in the receivership control of the governor (Yackle, 1989).

Ombudsmen are officials independent of prison administration, state government, and the courts. Based on Scandinavian practice, the ombudsmen system is used in several states (Connecticut, Kansas, Minnesota, New Jersey, Ohio, and South Carolina). Ombudsmen hear inmate complaints about illegal practices and conditions in the prison, conduct investigations, and settle disputes. Ombudsmen function more independently of prison officials than do masters and monitors, but present unsettled disputes to the court. Unlike masters and monitors, the ombudsmanship tends to become a permanent position (Rowat, 1986).

Human rights committees are designed to oversee prison compliance, with a variety of viewpoints and division of duties between members. The non-expert members are authorized to hire experts for assistance. Judge Johnson created a thirty-nine-member human rights committee in *Pugh v. Locke,* 406 F. Supp. 318 (M.D. Ala. 1976). On appeal, the Fifth Circuit Court of Appeals rejected the use of the lay human rights committee because there was no indication that the committee members were qualified by training or experience, *Pugh v. Locke,* 559 F. 2d 282, at 289 (5th Cir. 1977). The appeals court suggested the use of a single qualified master as a "more reasonable, less intrusive, more effective approach."

Expert panels keep all the benefits of a human rights committee, but add expertise. In a mental health institution case, *NYSARC v. Carey,* 357 F. Supp. 752; 393 F. Supp. 715 (E.D. N.Y., 1975), a court appointed an expert review panel of seven, with two chosen by the court, two by defendants, and three by plaintiffs, all experts in the field. The panel was given total access, a staff, and authority to make binding decisions. The panel, however, appeared too bureaucratic in its unresponsive and passive stance (Bradley and Clarke, 1976). As such, it has not been featured prominently in prison totality of conditions litigation.

In addition to fact-finding/oversight assistance, a court must design enforcement mechanisms in its remedial decrees. Courts commonly issue standards through court orders and give broad enforcement powers to a special master. Enforcement in equity may also include closing facilities, receivership, jurisdiction retained by court, and contempt citations.

Federal courts may ultimately close down prisons that are unfit for human habitation, either completely, *Gates v. Collier*, 423 F. Supp. 732, p. 743 (N.D. Miss. 1974), or partially, *Williams v. Wainwright*, 350 F. Supp. 33 (M.D. Fla. 1972). Most cases involve only the threat of closing down a prison, with intermediate steps in the case of failure to comply, as in *Battle v. Anderson*, 447 F. Supp. 516 (E.D. Okla. 1977). In such cases, courts have used their equity powers to order the release of numbers of inmates.

Receivership takes control of the prison away from those who appear to resist implementation and vests complete management authority with a receiver. Judge Johnson in *Newman v. Alabama*, 466 F. Supp. 628 (M.D. Ala., 1979), resorted to this severe remedy only after the presentation of overwhelming evidence of no genuine effort at compliance on the part of the Alabama Board of Corrections. Johnson rejected the appointment of a master and gave complete management control of the prison over to the receiver, Alabama governor Forrest H. James.

Jurisdiction retained by a court extends court involvement in prison reform through to its complete implementation. This enforcement mechanism is commonly used and is regarded as very intrusive in the daily administration of a prison. Courts will often retain jurisdiction for several years beyond initial reforms because prison authorities are not in full compliance. Retaining jurisdiction is frequently accompanied by an increase in supervision in order to monitor compliance (e.g., *Battle v. Anderson*, 447 F. Supp. 516 [E.D. Okla. 1977]). Prison officials often resent the court's "breathing down their necks" that seems to accompany jurisdiction retained (Harris and Spiller, 1976, p. 106).

Contempt citations are the conventional mechanisms used to enforce remedial decrees. In equity, the sanction is entirely up to the court, as judges have the discretion to determine what is necessary to bring the parties into compliance. Three defenses are typically raised by defendants in contempt citations: inability to comply, good faith effort to comply, and partial compliance. Inability to comply requires proof by the defendant of physical limits on actual ability. Lack of funds is not regarded as inability. Good faith effort to comply has been accepted by courts as a defense in which the defendant made efforts to remedy the problem, but was unable to do so because of a lack of state funds. Partial compliance will not prevent a court from issuing a contempt citation, but may help excuse noncompliance when combined with other defenses.

Post-Decree Phase: 1978–1986

Remedial decrees are refined, implemented, and evaluated in the post-decree phase. Enforcement mechanisms used by Judge Alaimo in the *Guthrie* case are typical of institutional reform litigation: special masters, special monitors, and jurisdiction retained with the threat of contempt citations. Because of the dynamic nature of remedy formulation by negotiation in *Guthrie*, some post-decree activities overlapped other phases of the litigation. For example, after complete racial integration was ordered on April 10, 1974, special masters Hutto, Tillman, and Thomas were appointed to oversee and report to Judge Alaimo on compliance, but only Hutto served in this brief role. As the parties prepared for litigation in 1974–78, Judge Alaimo appointed Special Master Pipkin from December 6, 1974, through his final report on October 8, 1979. While he was used primarily to assist the judge in assessing liability in various hearings, Pipkin also reported on the state of compliance with court orders regarding racial integration, inmate safety, and pressures on plaintiff-inmates in the litigation.

The comprehensive consent decrees of 1978 provided mechanisms for the defendants to report the state of their compliance. But in the spring of 1979, counsel for the plaintiffs and Judge Alaimo began to consider alternative methods of independently assessing implementation of the orders. Judge Alaimo may have been prompted by Governor Busbee's refusal to appoint an investigatory human rights committee (as in Alabama) or an ombudsman (*Atlanta Constitution*, 4/18/80). In March and April of 1979, counsel for defendants and plaintiffs discussed the possibility of appointing two new parties to assess compliance: the Civil Rights Division of the U.S. Department of Justice and a special monitor. The defendants' counsel, Georgia assistant attorneys general Walden and Kohler, objected to this expansion of parties and pointed out that the existing reporting mechanisms were sufficient.

Judge Alaimo, however, issued a court order on April 12, 1979, appointing the Civil Rights Division of the U.S. Department of Justice as *amicus curiae* "in order to assist the Court and the parties in assuring compliance with the Orders of this Court and in resolving all outstanding issues." Judge Alaimo also appointed the FBI to work with the U.S. DOJ civil rights division and specified that it "shall have the right to interview inmates and staff of Georgia State Prison and make such physical tours and inspections as are necessary to allow the Civil Rights Divisions . . . to participate in this matter and determine if the Orders . . . are being complied with." Judge Alaimo based this appointment on three factors: (1) the court expressly retained jurisdiction over the case, (2) the U.S. DOJ civil rights division had helped several courts in the U.S. Fifth Circuit in similar matters, and (3) as a U.S. district court, it was entitled to call upon the resources of the U.S. government, which had a stake in these public interests. The U.S. DOJ civil rights division, which was first involved as *amicus curiae* in the *Willowbrook* (mental health institution) case, had developed an extensive, expert knowledge of prison conditions, prison discipline, and medical and related reports.

The defendants did not formally object to the appointment of the *amicus curiae*, but questioned the further expansion of parties. Defendants asked if the appointment of the *amicus curiae* precluded a special monitor. They also asked if they would have input in a special monitor's nomination, function, and authority. The defendants also noted that certain *amicus curiae* attorneys were former members of plaintiffs' counsel (e.g., former LDF attorney Lynn Walker) and that they were concerned that the U.S. DOJ civil rights division was biased for the plaintiffs. On April 12, 1979, plaintiffs' counsel Bob Cullen offered recommendations for a special monitor and attached a proposed order of reference giving the monitor virtually unlimited access to any building or meeting held at Georgia State Prison, and any of its files or any files elsewhere. Cullen also proposed that the monitor have nearly complete operational control over the prison.

Judge Alaimo also took nominations from the defendants and included them with the plaintiff's list.[1]

Vincent Nathan, who was originally listed on the defendants' list of nominees, was appointed special monitor on June 1, 1979. He had served in a similar capacity at the Marion (Ohio) Correctional Institution in 1974 and the Lucas County Jail in Toledo, Ohio, in 1978–79 with the U.S. District Court, Northern District of Ohio, Western Division. Nathan was professor of law at the University of Toledo College of Law and specialized in commercial law. At forty, he left the university for the Toledo law offices of Cooper, Straub, Walinski & Cramer. On his first day with that organization, he received a letter from Judge Alaimo regarding his appointment as monitor at Reidsville.

The June 1, 1979, order of reference by Judge Alaimo essentially repeated the plaintiffs' proposals regarding the nearly unlimited authority of the special monitor to monitor compliance with, and implementation of, the relief ordered in the case. Special Monitor Nathan and his assistants were granted unlimited access to all facilities, buildings, and premises at GSP, and to all records and files at the prison or elsewhere. No advance notice was required except in emergencies. Nathan could conduct hearings on defendants' compliance on all related matters and was allowed to conduct confidential interviews at any time with any inmate, staff, or departmental employee. His authority included the power to hire additional personnel, fire current personnel, and transfer any staff as he deemed necessary, subject to court approval after defendants' written response. His authority also extended over the disposition of inmate grievances, quarterly written reports on the state of defendants' compliance, posting of the monitor's order of reference for inmates and staff, and provision of compensation, staff, office, equipment, and supplies by the defendants. Judge Alaimo also directed the defendants to post $25,000 with the court within thirty days of the order of reference to pay the initial costs of the special monitor.

The defendants objected strenuously to these processes. First, they asked for a new and much more limited order of reference. Second, they requested a stay on the June 1 order of reference—especially the requirement of posting $25,000 with the court for the monitor's expenses. Both motions were successful. A new order of reference, drafted by Judge Alaimo and Special Monitor Nathan, was issued on June 20. This order limited the authority and power of the special monitor. However, Nathan kept broad powers and control far beyond mere oversight of decree implementation, and continued to act as fact-finder, mediator, manager, and planner. His expenses and time were reimbursed by the defendants after assessments by the court. The new order of reference also redefined the role of the *amicus curiae*, the U.S. DOJ civil rights division, to limited assistance specifically requested and coordinated by the special monitor.[2]

From July through the fall of 1979 Special Monitor Nathan acquainted himself with GSP, the staff, consent decrees, and departmental rules, regulations, and procedures. He sought out sources of evidence and data for his first report to the court on the defendants' state of compliance. Many GSP staff and officials disliked Nathan's attitude from the start. Illustrative was Warden Balkcom's remark: "I didn't like Mr. Nathan. He came in like he was a secret investigator or something like that, rather than us working together to comply with the court orders" (Pollock, 1983, p. 97). This distrust intensified. GSP staff did not object to Nathan's use of environmental specialists to assess prison conditions, but they did object to his use of a polygraphist to gather evidence at their expense. The court allowed the use of an external polygraphist (order on 9/15/79), but ordered the results sealed and kept from all parties (including the special monitor) for possible admission into evidence at some future date. The defendants wanted their parallel polygraph exams done by an in-house polygraphist, with the results also sealed and kept with the special monitor's report. Plaintiffs' counsel objected and reached a compromise that allowed the defendants a confirming polygraph of those inmates examined by the monitor's polygraphist. The compromise also required the disclosure of the results of all polygraph exams as evidence. Judge Alaimo, Special Monitor Nathan, and counsel for the parties seemed increasingly adversarial at this time as Special Master Pipkin issued his final report on all remaining issues of fact in *Guthrie* on October 8, 1979.

Special Monitor Nathan issued a draft of his first report on the state of the defendants' compliance on November 20, 1979, after thirty days at Reidsville. He was accompanied at all times by Daniel R. Cron, a third-year law student at the University of Toledo College of Law. Nathan categorized legal requirements of the important remedial decrees into thirty groups.[3] In this report, he found essential compliance in only nine of the thirty categories. In all remaining areas, Nathan found some significant degree of noncompliance. He particularly noted the use of a restricted diet in disciplinary isolation and overcrowding, but reserved for later reports his assessment of three other areas: (1) effectiveness of the inmate grievance system, (2) racial discrimination in the administration of discipline, and (3) conditions in Building 2, an adjoining minimum security facility. Although the defendants objected that Building 2 was not expressly included in any remedial decrees in *Guthrie*, Nathan reasoned that it was essential because plaintiffs' counsel agreed to it.[4]

Plaintiffs' counsel immediately requested "extraordinary relief" of the court and asked for an order enjoining the restricted diet and closing all cells in disciplinary isolation within thirty days. This depended on a confirmation of the monitor's revised draft report. However, a rush to court ensued, with hearings from December 20 through 24, 1979, and January 3, 1980. These hearings featured testimony from two inmates, several engineers, a prison environmental expert, a plumbing contractor, Warden Balkcom, and Nathan. On January 7, Judge Alaimo issued a document entitled "Findings, Conclusions and Order" in which he enjoined further use of the restricted diet as discipline and the assignment of additional inmates to disciplinary isolation until compliance was achieved. He also ordered immediate improvement of the 280 cells in administrative segregation and disciplinary isolation (L and M buildings) within the next forty-five days (by 2/20/80), and threatened to close those units if the changes were not made. Alaimo declared in the order that "[t]his case will not end; but end it must! And so this Order's thrust is, perforce, toward that end." Certain of these improvements required considerable money not readily available to GSP or DOR. Acting quickly, the parties negotiated and on January 18 formally stipulated a modification of the judge's order. This gave the defendants time to obtain an emergency allocation from the Georgia state legislature, which quickly approved $741,000 to pay for basic structural changes.

Costs in *Guthrie* were beginning to mount. At this time, Steve Winter of the NAACP Legal Defense Fund presented the fund's bill for legal services in *Guthrie* to the Georgia attorney general's office. Although at least $1,421,209 in fees was established through December 1, 1979, the LDF was willing to settle for $950,000. The court finally ordered a fee of $650,000 after negotiations with the defendants, who had been ordered to pay all attorneys' fees for the plaintiffs. On January 18, 1980, defendant DOR Commissioner Evans also agreed to pay extra amounts to Nathan to enable Dan Cron to stay on, and to pay the fees of one of Nathan's law firm partners. The state had already begun construction, at a cost of $19,000,000, of a two-hundred-bed medium security medical corrections facility near Augusta for GSP inmates (*Augusta Chronicle*, 8/2/79, p. 1B). Furthermore, Henry S. Dogin of the U.S. Department of Justice informed Governor Busbee that federal Law Enforcement Assistance Administration funds would be cut off because there was no compliance effort demonstrated in *Guthrie*. Although this was stopped by calls from Nathan and Assistant U.S. Attorney General Paul Lawrence, the defendants were shocked by the expensive turn of events in *Guthrie*.

The defendants both agreed and disagreed with portions of the special monitor's draft report. However, they put aside their differences to avoid further delay in initiating appropriate changes at GSP. No formal objections were filed with Judge Alaimo, and non-budgetary improvements were immediately implemented. These included cleaning and painting disciplinary isolation cells, installing non-flammable mattresses, and ending restricted diets. The defendants also offered cost estimates for the necessary structural, plumbing, and mechanical renovations in disciplinary isolation and administration segregation. On February 25, 1980, the defendants formally stipulated a time schedule. Structural improvements began the next month with work on outdoor and indoor recreation areas, and schedules were set for the renovation of bunks, lighting, ventilation, fire safety devices, and inmates' personal property storage areas.

On February 1, 1980, Nathan filed a final version of the "First Report of the Special Monitor on the Defendants' State of Compliance." The defendants again refused to file formal objections to the report, although they disagreed with major portions of it. The defendants emphasized their genuine desire to cooperate with the monitor and all parties and to avoid further delays in the resolution of *Guthrie*. Because no objections were filed, Judge Alaimo issued an order on February 11 confirming the monitor's first report and directing the defendants to full compliance with all previous remedial decrees. The judge continued supervision of implementation by Special Monitor Nathan and directed additional supplemental compliance reports. Judge Alaimo continued this through the sixth report.

On February 14 Warden Balkcom was fired. Balkcom was frustrated with *Guthrie:* "I told them to take their little court orders and go someplace with it" (Pollock, 1983, p. 97). More importantly, Balcom could not stomach Nathan's personality and his scoldings. Balcom charged that Nathan only listened to half the story—the inmates' half. He thought that Nathan's interpretations of court orders were dangerous to both inmates and staff at GSP, and he refused to enforce the monitor's directives, convinced that violence would result if he did. Balcom received no sympathy from DOR officials or defendants' counsel; Evans said he had to let Balcom go because he would not enforce the court orders. Balcom gladly left, yet remained on friendly terms with DOR, where Commissioner Evans secured him a retirement pension.[5]

Assistant Commissioner Samuel Austin served as acting warden while DOR conducted a nationwide search for a new warden. Austin had worked on *Guthrie* from the beginning and had intimate knowledge of GSP, the remedial decrees, and Monitor Nathan. As acting warden, Austin worked on the problems identified in the monitor's first report and implemented the January 7, 1980, court order (and the February 25 modifications).[6] He also developed new inmate grievance procedures for allegations of physical and verbal abuse by staff.

On June 12, 1980, Governor Busbee and DOR Commissioner Evans announced the appointment of Charles M. Montgomery as the new warden of GSP, effective on July 1, 1980. Montgomery was unanimously chosen by the State Board of Offender Rehabilitation from a field of thirty applicants. He had sixteen years' federal corrections experience, which included a post as superintendent of the federal prison camp in Safford, Arizona. On loan from the Federal Bureau of Prisons, Montgomery assumed his responsibilities on July 7 and immediately commissioned a comprehensive security analysis of GSP from the National Institute of Corrections. He also implemented new administrative policies and procedures.

Nathan filed his second report on October 26, 1980. This focused on Building 2, a facility located across the main highway from GSP. Building 2 consisted of a single minimum security building and four trailers that housed between 350 and 380 men. These men staffed the outside work details, including the dairy, hog barn, and feed mill, and maintained livestock. Although he didn't include Building 2 in his first report, Nathan reasoned that it was so closely connected to GSP that, although never expressly included in *Guthrie*, it must also comply with all provisions of the remedial decrees. Building 2 was excepted only from certain maximum security renovations and administrative segregation conditions stipulated for GSP. Based on information Dan Cron compiled in the spring and early summer of 1980, the second report directed certain renovations in Building 2 until it was replaced. While defendants' counsel formally objected, they later withdrew their objections (December 7, 1980).

At GSP, some of the old-school staff began openly to resist Warden Montgomery and the changes brought by *Guthrie*. They thought that the new administration and procedures threatened established ways of doing things at GSP and were suspicious of the warden's close relationship with the monitor. In short, Montgomery was another outside threat. Morale at GSP fell further when, with the assistance of a guard, four death row inmates escaped on July 28, 1980.

Subsequently, DOR discontinued the distribution of free tobacco to inmates. This resulted in widespread work stoppage on October 31 by inmates, with correctional officers and supervisors following suit. Protesting staff stopped work for three hours so that the first shift had to keep the entire inmate population locked down with no food or work details permitted (*Atlanta Constitution*, 12/22/80). Although staff returned to work, opposition to the new administration grew. Guards, especially, protested that Montgomery wouldn't let them use force against inmates under any circumstances, even self-protection. DOR Commissioner Evans reorganized operational procedures to provide greater state-level scrutiny of decisions at GSP, while Governor Busbee sent a letter to Evans warning about the consequences of strikes and work stoppages:

> Any thought by any misguided dissident that his disruptive and undermining activity will change my support of you [Commissioner Evans] and the Warden [Montgomery] is the most pitiful form of wishful thinking. . . . I have spoken with the Attorney General today, and we feel that the law is clear in Georgia Code Annotated 89–1302 that slowdowns, work stoppages and other attempts to hinder the operations of the institutions are grounds for dismissal. Those engaging in such activity will be dismissed, and appeals of dismissals will be fought with every resource at our command. (Monitor's Third Report, p. 6)

At this time, Warden Montgomery hired two new assistant wardens from the Federal Bureau of Prisons, Jerry Thomas and Aaron

Brown. He also converted GSP to new unit management coordination of four small units. The monitor applauded these state-level efforts to impose greater accountability on activities at GSP and reported genuine hope for compliance with such a strong showing by the defendants.

One very important, yet scarcely noticed, reform by Warden Montgomery took place about this time. Death row was moved from the fifth floor of the main building at GSP to the Georgia Diagnostic and Classification Center in Jackson (*Atlanta Chronicle*, 12/22/80). At its previous location, death row had been a focal point for all GSP inmates wherever they were in the prison. Its effect was reflected in the increased security and administration problems at times of impending executions.

The third report of the special monitor, issued December 31, 1980, addressed the general state of compliance at GSP and Building 2. Nathan commented favorably on the changes in leadership at GSP and the chain of command within DOR. While he found a continuing lack of compliance in many areas, he was optimistic that a state of genuine and continuing cooperation between parties had been achieved with changes in GSP leadership and DOR operational procedures: "In the opinion of the Special Monitor these steps will promote the joint objective of the defendants, the plaintiffs, and the Court that full compliance be achieved with the Court's mandates in the case as speedily as possible" (pp. 7–8).

Curiously, it was plaintiffs' counsel who objected, in part, to the special monitor's third report. Though highly critical of conditions in Building H, Nathan noted improvements and recommended fans and other simple ventilation renovations. Attorneys Cullen and Winter, however, thought that Nathan's report was invalid in that he did not base his recommendation on the advice of a sanitation expert. Defendants' counsel supported the monitor and argued that Nathan had discretion to appoint experts as needed. They also pointed out that there was no showing that the special monitor was unqualified to observe sanitary conditions.

Warden Montgomery worked as an intermediary between the defendants and the monitor from 1980 to 1982. Nathan was generally positive about Montgomery's role, but GSP staff and state politicians were not confident that he represented their interests. Montgomery had fired over one hundred staff members of GSP and was perceived by many as an interloper who hid in his office and never walked the halls (*Atlanta Constitution*, 12/22/80). State Representative Joseph Kennedy (D-Claxton), chairman of the Prisons subcommittee, was openly hostile to Warden Montgomery (*Atlanta Journal*, 4/12/82, p. 1A). In response, DOR appeared to take the heat off Montgomery by assigning Assistant Commissioner Samuel Austin as full-time chief liaison between DOR and Monitor Nathan, beginning August 1981. On August 16, 1981, DOR shifted Lanson Newsome, then-warden of the Macon Correctional Institution, to GSP as on-site project director for compliance with *Guthrie* orders. It was unofficially understood, however, that Newsome was sent to replace Warden Montgomery. Later, Montgomery did receive an official vote of confidence by Judge Alaimo, Monitor Nathan, Governor Busbee, and Commissioner Evans, and his contract was extended for a second year.

Defendants' counsel experienced important changes during the summer of 1981. Michael J. Bowers, a native of Commerce, Georgia, became Georgia's attorney general. Concerned about the shambles at GSP, he wondered how the state ever got involved in such an ever-expanding lawsuit as *Guthrie*. Bowers became more involved in *Guthrie* than his predecessor and assigned a more aggressive assistant attorney general, John C. Jones, to the case. A native of Washington state and a graduate of Georgia Tech and Mercer University's law school, Jones assessed Nathan as some sort of pro-plaintiff-inmate counsel, and treated him accordingly. Jones's perception of Nathan may have been accurate; others have since described plans that Nathan put together with Cullen and Winter (e.g., Levinson, 1982, p. 10). However, Jones was able to gain Montgomery's confidence and worked closely with him in spite of Nathan.

The fourth report of the monitor was issued November 2, 1981. Nathan assessed the defendants' state of compliance with *Guthrie* orders in twenty-eight major areas and found substantial compliance in several. Nathan and Judge Alaimo had taken a surprise tour of GSP before the issuance of the fourth report. Although there were numerous threats on their lives and a homemade bomb was discovered shortly before their arrival, they were favorably impressed by the security and improving conditions at the prison (*Atlanta Journal*, 7/22/81). On March 10, 1981, Alaimo ordered a complete list of the remaining issues in *Guthrie* and a timetable for the resolution of those issues. In response, Nathan developed a very general list of remaining issues, with no timetable for implementation. However, Nathan developed a compendium of all orders in *Guthrie* and reported his optimism that problems at GSP itemized in his fourth report would be corrected by June 1, 1982. He also indicated his hope that complete compliance in all remaining issues would be achieved by January 1, 1983, stating, "Commissioner Evans and Warden Montgomery have set a course of action that is calculated to achieve substantial compliance with all of the Court's orders in this case in the relatively near future" (p. 445).

On February 18, 1982, Judge Alaimo, with Nathan's recommendation, issued an order closing M Building, which housed inmates in administrative segregation and disciplinary isolation. Deteriorating environmental conditions made the building unfit for human habitation. Most interesting was Judge Alaimo's contempt of court sanction based on the defendants' written admission that they had violated court orders. Normally reserved to compel compliance by uncooperative parties, this sanction was applied to defendants who were not only trying to comply but acknowledging their own noncompliance. In response, Commissioner Evans ordered Montgomery to place greater emphasis on environmental sanitation, at least at a level equal with the other compliance issues in *Guthrie*. Judge Alaimo did not order the building opened until March 8, 1983.

On June 1, 1982, Lanson Newsome was appointed warden of GSP. Newsome's father was a guard at GSP who raised his family on GSP property. Newsome started as a guard at GSP in 1964, straight out of high school. He worked his way up through the Georgia corrections system and earned degrees at various colleges (Andrew College, Georgia Southern College, and the University of Georgia). Newsome had served as deputy warden and warden at several Georgia correctional institutions before coming to GSP as project director of *Guthrie* and understudy to Warden Montgomery. At the time of his appointment, Newsome was the youngest warden in the state and may have been the youngest of any maximum security prison in the country (*Atlanta Journal*, 6/28/82). Montgomery stayed on at GSP until July 1, to ensure a smooth transition. Louise Clifton, who had worked with *Guthrie* since its initiation, remained as Warden Newsome's executive assistant in relations with the judge, special monitor, attorneys, and DOR and state officials. Newsome proved his leadership after less than six months on the job, accepting responsibility for excessive use of force by guards at GSP. His ten-day disciplinary salary suspension stemmed from a review finding twenty-nine incidents of excessive use of force by guards (*Macon Telegraph & News*, 11/24/82).

Judge Alaimo seemed happy with the progress in *Guthrie* and issued an important order on July 14, 1982, in which he disclosed his expectations that: (1) the monitorship would end on June 1, 1983, (2) the special monitor would issue a final compliance report by August 1, 1983, and (3) if the report reflected substantial compliance with the remedial decrees in *Guthrie*, the case would be reduced to a final injunctive order. The judge also agreed with the defendants on the need to stop the expansion of the lawsuit. He directed the special monitor to design detailed self-audit documents for GSP, as had been previously ordered by the court on January 15, 1982. However, Judge Alaimo threatened to impose punitive coercive measures (e.g., receivership or expansion of plaintiffs' counsel) if there was no substantial compliance by defendants.

In the monitor's fifth report, issued December 1, 1982, Nathan found substantial noncompliance and seemed noticeably less optimistic about reform. The list of directives now included over 2,500 items for compliance, and the state legislature seemed reluctant to spend more money on GSP. Staff and officials felt overloaded by the expansion of remedial decrees. DOR Commissioner Evans commented, "You'd be working on one thing, and they'd come out with a bunch of new orders, [and] it has made things difficult" (*Atlanta Journal*, 12/30/82, p. 14A). Also, the perspective of defendants' counsel changed; they were more argumentative and alleged that Nathan had changed the standards and scope of remedies in *Guthrie*. Previously, they had never filed formal objections when they disputed the monitor's assertion of fact. Now, the defendants claimed that Nathan falsely reported noncompliance at GSP when conditions had actually improved. The Georgia legislature also became more disputatious; it objected to Nathan's part-time fees, which exceeded the full-time salary of the governor, exclusive of expenses and assistants (Levinson, 1982). Although the monitor's fifth report was unfavorable, the judge imposed no punitive coercive measures. Judge Alaimo may also have had some questions about Nathan's credibility.

Violence and security problems remained with GSP in 1982, as well as a restlessness that accompanied the bustle of renovation under

Project 360. During the year, six inmates were killed, there was a rash of escapes (fourteen on one day, December 3), and staff misconduct continued. Nathan and the defendants were busy blaming one another in the media for these mishaps. The defendants blamed the court-ordered (Nathan) purging of inmates' records in 1980 for eased security rankings for a number of volatile inmates who escaped. Nathan countered that the records were purged twenty months before the escapes, and blamed the escapes on the defendants' noncompliance with the remedial decrees concerning the inmates' physical protection. Inmates blamed the monitor and court for the increased violence, which they believed justified the breakouts (e.g., *Atlanta Journal & Constitution*, 8/3/30). Other state officials attributed the violence and rash of escapes to the major construction work being done and the inexperience of the staff. These same officials blamed the court-ordered remedies for some degree of the unrest. Staff at GSP continued to use excessive force in handling the inmates, and were often angry and frustrated when reprimanded or fired for their actions. Warden Newsome blamed much of the unrest on "[c]hanges coming so swift. . . . A lot of officers don't understand the changes" (*Atlanta Journal*, 9/19/82, pp. 1A, 10A).

Between January and June of 1983, the parties met frequently and negotiated many of the remaining issues of compliance. The most significant stipulation involved security upgrade of GSP, which included the employment of 110 new correctional officers, and the use of metal detectors and security items (e.g., body alarms)—all at an estimated cost of $7,700,000. The parties also stipulated to the defendants' "Comprehensive Plan for Vocational, Academic and Rehabilitation Programs for Georgia State Prison" (1/20/83), "Inmate Personal Property Losses and Claims Report" (4/13/83), "Mental Health/Mental Retardation Plan" (4/25/83), "Inmate Discipline" (6/2/83), the monitor's "Audit Document" (6/16/83), "Temporary Use of Handcuffs on Special Management Unit Inmates in M-Building" (6/16/83), and "Institution-Wide Incentive Plan" (6/16/83). Finally, an audit document for the defendants' self-audit was submitted by Nathan, revised, and ordered by Alaimo on August 31, 1983.

Resistance to Special Monitor Nathan grew more intense and personal during 1983. The *Augusta Chronicle* (1/26/83) declared Nathan "Georgia's Highest Paid Employee" at $75.00 an hour. Nathan had submitted legal fees of almost $600,000. This included his time, per

diem expenses, and the costs of assistants and experts. During legislative budget hearings, State Senator Wayne Garner (D-Carrollton)
observed, "In light of that, I fail to understand [what incentive Nathan
would have] to help us get out from under the court order" (*Augusta
Chronicle*, 1/26/83).

Nathan again found substantial noncompliance in his sixth report,
issued September 1, 1983. Completed with the assistance of Judith
Heck and Frederick Byers, the report was Nathan's most comprehensive, but it did not include any assessment of the mental health and
mental retardation plan and of conditions in Building 2, scheduled
for closing on the date of the sixth, and final, report. Nathan and his
staff tried to use the audit documents prepared with the fifth report,
but found them impossible to use. Furthermore, Nathan did not consider useful or reliable the audit documents completed by the defendants. Thus, the sixth report consisted of narrative reports outlining
the defendants' state of compliance in terms of compliance, compliance with exceptions, noncompliance, and no finding. Nathan
relied on many experts for this and previous reports, including Samuel W. Hoover (sanitation), Harry Markel and John Hulla (industrial
health and safety), Dr. Lambert King and Dr. Jay Harness (medical),
Dr. Naomi Goldstein and Dr. Henry Weinstein (mental health), and Dr.
Seth Hirshorn (disciplinary procedures). In his conclusion, Nathan
admitted that GSP had come a long way since his first report, but he
still found substantial noncompliance in nearly every area specified
in the court-ordered audit document. His recommendation strongly
implied that Judge Alaimo ought to impose punitive coercive measures on the defendants.

In 1983, Vincent Nathan left GSP for Texas, where he had already
begun his duties as special master under Judge William Justice in the
reform of the Texas prison system.[7] Governor Joe Frank Harris called
the end of the four-year court monitorship a milestone event and
noted that the state had paid the monitor and his staff $871,000.
While Alaimo refused to grant the defendants' motion to dismiss the
lawsuit, Governor Harris was proud that "Judge Alaimo has seen fit to
let us run our prisons" (*Atlanta Constitution*, 12/8/83). Steve Winter
also left the *Guthrie* case at this time to work with death sentence
cases for the LDF. Plaintiffs' counsel brought on Martha Miller as a
replacement who acted as plaintiffs' monitor and assisted in the case.
Miller had worked with Cullen in the Augusta office of the Georgia

Legal Services Corporation. She also assisted Cullen in the continuing negotiations in *Guthrie* through 1986.

The negotiations and renovation at GSP continued through 1985,
with personal reports from the negotiators to Judge Alaimo. The new
Rogers facility replaced the old Building 2. The total redevelopment
of GSP was finally completed in 1985. Also nearing an end were the
tiring negotiation sessions held since the late 1970s. But some issues
were still unresolved. Negotiators included plaintiffs' attorneys Cullen and Miller, while the defendants' team included attorneys Jones,
Walden, and Daryl A. Robinson, as well as Austin, Newsome, and
Clifton. Daryl Robinson, an undergraduate and law graduate of the
University of Georgia, was assigned as the senior assistant attorney
general responsible for the criminal division, which included *Guthrie*
and other cases against DOR. John Walden had been director of the
division before January 1984, but was kept on as special prosecutor to
maintain continuity in the negotiations.

Conditions and procedures at GSP were noticeably changed by
1984. The *Macon Telegraph & News* (2/12/84) reported "At Last: A
Little Law & Order Behind Bars" and praised the much-improved
conditions at GSP with an analogy: "Just as Yank [an inmate] had to
do to get back his floor (stripping old wax), Warden Newsome is having to strip away layers of misuse and neglect to reclaim his prison."
There had been no killings at GSP since October 1982. From 3,200
inmates and 306 correctional officers in 1976, GSP now held an average of 1,503 inmates with over one thousand guards. Warden Newsome took over the prison one unit at a time, beginning with the mess
hall, then the recreation areas, and finally the cell blocks. In the
process, he fired 251 staff and disciplined over 350 prison employees.
GSP had become a model prison, studied by visiting correctional
administrators from Alabama, Louisiana, and other prison systems
(*Atlanta Journal & Constitution*, 1/13/85, pp. 1B, 8B).[8]

Meanwhile, Judge Alaimo grew tired of the negotiations over the
endless details. He wanted to end the lawsuit and issue a final permanent injunction, if the parties would only stop dragging their feet.
The defendants were slow but, in the end, acquiescent, and agreed to
the demands of a constitutional prison. The plaintiffs seemed to exac-
erbate matters by continually adding new issues and details. Further,
plaintiffs' counsel obviously benefited by prolonging the *Guthrie* litigation with additional fees and authority over GSP.

From February 1984 to June 1985, Independent Monitor Charles Bell was appointed by Judge Alaimo to follow the case through to complete implementation. A graduate of Morehouse College and the law school at Vanderbilt University, Bell was an administrative hearing officer in equal employment opportunity cases at DOR before working on *Guthrie*. While plaintiffs' counsel expressed doubt about Bell's objectivity as a DOR employee, they consented to his appointment and later commented that his report was fair.

Monitor Bell's approach differed markedly from Nathan's. While Nathan would surprise the defendants by waiting to notify them of potential problems in his reports, Bell would tell them immediately. Bell issued a monitor's report on June 1, 1985, on the newly constructed, minimum security Rogers facility. Bell found minimum compliance at Rogers. Everyone seemed satisfied with the results of Bell's monitorship.

Upon receipt of Bell's report, Judge Alaimo made a surprise visit to GSP to view the conditions. He was especially impressed with the new Rogers facility. Alaimo formally approved the report of Independent Monitor Bell and called on the parties to prepare for the final permanent injunction. The end of *Guthrie* was in sight.

A final injunctive order was issued by Judge Alaimo on June 26, 1985, in a hurriedly called session in the new hearing room in the east wing of GSP. Alaimo enjoined the defendants from failing or refusing to comply with all consent decrees and orders, specifying the compendium of orders previously collected by Monitor Nathan, as well as all other remedial decrees. He threatened that any failure to comply would result in various sanctions, such as contempt, imposition of fines, and "other appropriate remedies." He also kept plaintiffs' counsel on for one extra year to further monitor compliance with the final permanent injunction. Finally, Alaimo ordered the defendants pay the plaintiffs' legal fees, subject to documentation and defendants' right to challenge, as well as fees to plaintiffs' counsel for the next twelve months. Governor Joe Frank Harris commented, "We are free now to operate Georgia State Prison without federal court intervention, although we are bound forever to the requirements agreed upon under *Guthrie*."

Plaintiffs' counsel monitored compliance with the remedial decrees in *Guthrie* over the next twelve months. Early during this period, plaintiffs' counsel voiced concern over the possible violation of *Guth-*

rie orders when an inmate in disciplinary isolation, Ray Sharp, was shot and killed by a guard during an attempted escape. However, Alaimo did not construe this as related to the *Guthrie* orders. Plaintiffs' counsel Bob Cullen estimated the attorneys' fees for the Georgia Legal Services Corporation for work done on *Guthrie* from 1978 through 1986 to be over $3,000,000, with over $1,100,000 incurred before 1982. Estimates by the state of Georgia ranged from $55,000,000 to well over $100,000,000 in state funds for structural changes at GSP during the *Guthrie* case (*Atlanta Constitution*, 6/27/85; *Florida Times-Union*, 6/27/85; *Savannah Morning News*, 6/27/87).

6

Power and Personal
Perspectives in *Guthrie*

This chapter offers an analysis of the *Guthrie* litigation, with emphasis on the key decision-makers and how they perceived the case and underlying issues. The analysis relies on descriptions of comparative cases in the literature and the archival data in *Guthrie*, but most extensively on data gathered in focused interviews with key decision-makers in *Guthrie*. Respondents are not identified. This results from a necessary compromise between the need to disclose all identities to demonstrate a chain of evidence, and the ethical need to protect individuals and to avoid affecting the participants' subsequent activities.

Power in Prison Reform Litigation

Most knowledge of prison reform litigation has depended on the opinions published by judges in legal cases. The secondary literature surrounding these cases typically examines only the personality of the judge (e.g., Kennedy, 1978). While other studies include details on the relations of public officials with a judge (e.g., Yarbrough, 1981), the existing literature focuses nearly all of its attention on the judge and judicial capacity, legitimacy, or managerial abilities. These sources provide an introduction and overview to institutional reform litigation, but tend to narrow our focus on the judge as the key decision-maker.

There are excellent biographical and personality studies of judges (e.g., Yarbrough, 1981) and prison officials (e.g., Jacobs, 1977) involved in prison reform litigation. These studies may be too narrow for present purposes, however, as the influence and interaction of many key decision-makers are simply not examined. For example, participant observations within the prison assess the wardens (e.g., Jacobs, 1977), with little attention to court actors. Life histories of the judge (e.g., Yarbrough, 1981) or other court actors neglect prison and state administrators. Clearly, a systematic understanding of institutional reform litigation would include the personalities of a combination of key decision-makers: prison officials, state bureaucrats, attorneys, judges, masters, and others (e.g., Crouch and Marquart, 1990; Yackle, 1989). Such an understanding makes it necessary to examine these personalities over the entire length of the litigation and not simply at the point of compliance (e.g., Cooper, 1988). For example, administrators may at first welcome the judicial decree as a way to argue for more state funds or as a protection from executive interference. However, their attitudes may later turn sour when the courts retain jurisdiction and extend their attention to daily prison operations, as in Arkansas (Harris and Spiller, 1976, p. 105).

Personal Perspectives in *Guthrie*

From this study of *Guthrie*, it is evident that there are many key decision-makers in institutional reform litigation. They hold different positions, and not all of them are legally trained. To understand such litigation, it is necessary to look beyond the judge to the administrators, inmates, attorneys for both parties, and a variety of court-appointed personnel. Even to assume that the judge is the central figure in institutional reform litigation may not be accurate. It is true that at certain points in the *Guthrie* litigation Judge Alaimo was the focal point, leading the case toward resolution. But these occasions were rare. More typically, the judge deferred resolution of the issues to the parties' attorneys in negotiated settlements or to court-appointed officials. In fact, the day-to-day control of the court-ordered mediation, hearings, and monitorship was placed almost entirely in the hands of court-appointed personnel, and retrieved by Judge Alaimo only after he insisted on ending the litigation and after these other key decision-makers acquiesced. Judge Alaimo maintained a symbolic role throughout the litigation as a sort of catalyst for change (Moss, 1985) on those occasions when mediation or negotiation failed, as well as a scapegoat for criticism of the case by the media and public.

But the litigation was actually driven by a larger set of key decision-makers.

At least thirty-six key decision-makers were identified in *Guthrie* from archival and interview analyses. Of these, none were drawn from the large group of plaintiff-inmates. Even the namesake of the lawsuit, Arthur S. Guthrie, quickly disappeared in the archives and the memories of those involved. Some key decision-makers had no knowledge of Guthrie, although others remarked that they had heard Guthrie was back in the Georgia correctional system after parole release from GSP. The lack of even one key decision-making plaintiff-inmate directly affected by the changes from *Guthrie* dramatically points out how the polycentric institutional reform case differs from ordinary civil litigation. In the latter, cases depend on the decisions of the disputing parties, especially the plaintiff (Trubeck et al., 1987). Yet the plaintiff-inmates in *Guthrie* were sometimes so invisible to the key decision-makers that they complained that for three years they were not even informed of the progress on their own case (e.g., Lumumba, 1979). The plaintiff-inmates questioned whether plaintiffs' counsel was working for them or for the court, with the more aggressive inmates urging others to ignore the lawsuit and make their own changes: "All the so-called do-gooders and the professionals are mere novices compared to the average convict, so if things are to change, we the inmates and convicts had better get in a position to insure that the changes will be for our benefit . . . not for the benefit of . . . some high-paid 'professional' criminologist" (anonymous, *Prison Union Notice* (GSP), 1/5/78).

Key decision-makers were found in the other groups in *Guthrie*: the court, defendants, defendants' counsel, and plaintiffs' counsel. Key decision-makers among the court included Judge Alaimo, the mediator, a representative of the U.S. Department of Justice *amicus curiae*, one special master, the special monitor, and the independent monitor. Key defendants included DOR commissioners, one assistant commissioner, two planners in the governor's office of planning and budget, six wardens at GSP, and one executive assistant to the GSP wardens. Defendants' key counsel included David J. Bailey, Dorothy Beasley, Arthur Bolton, Michael Bowers, Richard Chambers, John C. Jones, David L. G. King, Harrison Kohler, Don A. Langham, Daryl Robinson, and John C. Walden. Attorneys associated with the NAACP Legal Defense Fund and Georgia Legal Services figured prominently among plaintiffs' counsel. Refer to appendix E for the entire pool of those involved in the *Guthrie* litigation and those identified as key decision-makers from the archival and interview data.

Twelve self-perceived positions were taken by key decision-makers in the *Guthrie* case. These positions included judge, mediator, GSP administrator, DOR administrator, state budget office, state attorney general administrator, plaintiffs' counsel-litigator, plaintiffs' counsel-negotiator, defendants' counsel-litigator, defendants' counsel-negotiator, *amicus curiae*, and those not extensively involved in *Guthrie*. While five of the key decision-makers interviewed did not perceive themselves as significantly involved in *Guthrie*, the archives and perceptions of others attest to their importance in the case.

Three key decision-makers perceived their part in *Guthrie* as essentially judicial, characterized by neutrality toward the parties and ultimate control over the case. Court-appointed officials in *Guthrie* generally shared this self-perceived part with the judiciary. But not all appointed officials perceived themselves as judicial. Two of the four court-appointed officials perceived themselves as judicial, with some degree of ultimate control over the case. The other two appointments perceived themselves in other roles, answering to and leaving all ultimate control to another. Four key decision-makers described their role as mediator. Perceptions of the mediator part involved, in all instances, a dedication to non-adversarial dispute resolution of the issues in *Guthrie*. It also involved some degree of neutrality between parties, but placed ultimate control in the hands of the parties or judge. Of these four subjects, the two individuals active in *Guthrie* during formal mediation attempts (1973–74) still assert that mediation would have worked. Other subjects generally shared this belief, except for some of the self-perceived litigators.

The GSP administrator position was often described in terms of a compliance manager and was adopted by four of the key decision-makers interviewed. Managing compliance at GSP took place on many levels. While it was not possible to interview a large number of the staff at GSP, an extensive tour of the facilities suggested that many of those not formally interviewed, from assistant wardens to guards and kitchen staff, shared this perception of their part in *Guthrie*. In this instance, their professional attitude toward their work suggested that managing compliance was the job of every employee at GSP.

Three key decision-makers perceived themselves as central office administrators at the Georgia Department of Offender Rehabilitation during *Guthrie*. In this role, they coordinated both negotiation and compliance in the case and sought funding from state political leaders. They were very busy, juggling their time between *Guthrie* and the problems of other state correctional facilities. The massive and controversial nature of *Guthrie* often brought them to the attention of political leaders in executive and legislative branches in state government.

Two key decision-makers saw themselves as part of the governor's budget office, which directed funds to GSP. Their contact with the legal proceedings was remote, but they interacted substantially with DOR, GSP, and other state officials. Not surprisingly, these key decision-makers tended to view governors (Busbee, Harris) as the central decision-makers in the *Guthrie* case.

Six of those interviewed functioned as counsel for the plaintiff-inmates, and obviously perceived themselves accordingly. Of these six, two viewed themselves as litigators, taking a firm adversarial stance to the defendants' position. Their activities in *Guthrie* included drafting complaint-briefs and interrogatories and conducting discovery proceedings and hearings. Four viewed themselves as negotiators, arranging terms with the defendants (and their counsel) for consent remedial decrees and stipulations. They did not meet with the judge in open court except for judicial approval of the consent decrees and stipulations.

Eight of those interviewed served as counsel for the defendant-state and described their positions accordingly. Two viewed their task as administrators of the *Guthrie* case within the Georgia attorney general's office. They supervised, selected, and supported assistant attorneys general as policy directions on *Guthrie* changed (i.e., mediate, litigate, negotiate, litigate). Three assistant attorneys general viewed themselves as litigators, expecting to fight the plaintiffs' counsel all the way on every issue in controversy. The remaining three assistant attorneys general saw themselves as negotiators, stipulating to and arranging terms to resolve the dispute in *Guthrie*.

One of the key decision-makers interviewed served as *amicus curiae*. While essentially advocating the rights of the plaintiff-inmates, this person represented the interests of the U.S. government concerning constitutional conditions and practices in state prisons.

During the fourteen years of the *Guthrie* litigation, various subgroups made up different triads that included members of the court, plaintiffs' counsel, and defendants and their counsel. This gave the case a generational effect, where parties implemented and monitored remedial decrees designed by earlier litigants in the case. Different generations of litigation teams would often have little knowledge of what the earlier participants had done or who had designed the remedial decree under review. The years of litigation, combined with this generational effect, appeared to cause Judge Alaimo and the few others who were with *Guthrie* from the beginning to completely forget earlier activities. No key decision-maker recalled Joseph Coggins II, or that he had authored the original complaint. And memories of the years spent in mediation were wistful at best ("Should have let mediation go on longer").

Over the course of the litigation, key decision-makers in the same position played their roles very differently. For example, while early defendants' counsel played the role of mediator ("we negotiated everything"), changes in the attorney general's office resulted in more aggressively pursued pre-trial discovery designed to go all the way to the Supreme Court ("[Attorney General] Bowers wanted a mean attorney"). The litigation strategies of mediation, pre-trial discovery, hearings, negotiations, and implementation are marked by corresponding changes in plaintiffs' and defendants' counsel, defendants (wardens, commissioners, etc.), and court-appointed personnel. While some scholars have noted the polycentric nature of institutional reform litigation (e.g., Fuller, 1978), they have focused on the large number of individuals affected at the conclusion of the litigation. This more dynamic case study reveals that *Guthrie* was actually a set of separately staged lawsuits linked abstractly by a common concern with conditions and practices at GSP. This generational effect may be unique to institutional reform litigation and may contribute to the protracted, complex, and highly stressful nature of this type of lawsuit.

In most instances, the fast turnover of personnel seemed due to burn-out. While some personnel moved on from *Guthrie* to more personally attractive positions, all key decision-makers were affected by the intense pressure associated with the case. Litigation was extremely complex (growing from 7 issues to over 2,500), involved the coordination of many lives, and offered no relief in sight for most of its fourteen years. One key decision-maker commented that stress and burn-out may have been the greatest problem in *Guthrie*: "Extremely high stress; you can't count up the stress problem . . . and GSP employees [felt] they couldn't leave because there were no other employers in Reidsville."

The judicialization (Rosenbloom, 1983) of procedures and practices at GSP related directly to the high turnover of prison officials and staff who found the remedial decrees too voluminous to assimilate even after they were condensed and published for all employees. One interviewee noted the "extraordinary paperwork . . . extraordinary pressure on staff and inmates . . . with no relief in sight for anyone." Even the level of violence among inmates and between inmates and staff at GSP may have been associated with the high turnover of staff during the lawsuit, according to several key decision-makers who pointed to "tremendous tension between Black and White inmates used by Guards to control GSP." The old-boy network of GSP staff that remained passed on the old-fashioned way of doing things because they could not understand the compendium, compilation, and innumerable posted orders in *Guthrie*. Additionally, while there was no trial or appeal, adversarial relations between litigants in mediation, pre-trial discovery, negotiations, and implementation were often quite personal and antagonistic. Some key decision-makers believed there would have been less pressure and violence had the case simply gone to trial. Others speculated that these pressures may have played an important part in obtaining a permanent injunction from those tired of the fourteen-year lawsuit.

In interviews, respondents indicated that the most important individuals in the lawsuit were Judge Alaimo, Special Monitor Nathan, and Warden Newsome. Respondents were intense and blunt in assessing the contributions of these three. Significantly ranked above the others, Judge Alaimo and Monitor Nathan tied as standouts, but received quite different assessments from other key decision-makers in the case.

Judge Alaimo received almost unanimous praise for his role in the development of *Guthrie*. One detractor was convinced that the judge was "simply after publicity" in the case. But all others interviewed wished that Judge Alaimo had been more active: "If we did it over there would have been no monitorship—make the judge do it himself." This seems unusual, since three of the seven urging a greater role for Judge Alaimo were clearly aligned with the defendant-state during the case. However, these members of the defendants group argued that the greater evils of the special monitor could have been avoided if Judge Alaimo had taken more personal control over *Guthrie*. Additionally, some defendant-state group members had considerable respect for Alaimo's character and work (e.g., "outstanding quality of intellect—[he] cut through the issues"), and hoped he would direct the litigation.

Monitor Nathan received mixed assessments of his involvement in *Guthrie*. Not surprisingly, all critics were drawn from the ranks of the defendants, while supporters were drawn from plaintiffs' counsel, defendants, and court groups. Four key decision-makers described Nathan's role positively, one even calling the federal monitor a "pivotal figure." These respondents argued that the state would never have changed its procedures without Nathan's prodding: "[He was] more imposing and influential than even the Commissioner." Some went even further to say that Monitor Nathan did a "brilliant job" and that he was "respected by all parties" in the case. At least four key decision-makers, however, disagreed. "The number one problem in *Guthrie* was Nathan!" one declared emphatically. Four complained of Nathan's intrusion into prison operations: "[H]e thought he was the judge—the evil despot—[he was on an] ego trip, a social experiment." Three interviewees blamed the monitor for much of the violence at GSP, arguing that as a result of Nathan's intrusions, inmates "knew there was no discipline so they disrupted." One critic charged that in specific cases Monitor Nathan was "responsible for a tremendous loss of human life and suffering." Finally, one critic summed up the larger impact of Nathan on prison reform in Georgia:

> [He took a] highly adversarial posture at the beginning; Nathan came on as "see all, know all" and nobody had any sense . . . Nathan antagonized the State government executives and legislators who would get upset at Nathan and wouldn't give money . . . Nathan's reports gave Georgia a bad press nationally . . . you can't separate the issues from the personality of Nathan . . . [he] prompted antagonisms within the system.

Warden Newsome was assessed positively by all. Those who rated him as the most important key decision-maker in the case included three defendants and one attorney. Newsome was perceived as important because he directed the final compliance at GSP. Nearly every key decision-maker recognized at least minimal compliance at GSP under him. Only those who had not kept current in the case were unsure of the level of compliance at GSP under his guidance. These assessments of Newsome also remarked on his character and his ability to manage the staff and inmates at GSP.

Newsome's ability as a manager and leader appears to be a significant factor in the final compliance to *Guthrie*. The sudden changes he brought to GSP staff were noted by several key decision-makers: "no blue jeans; officers wore ties; and no drunks." Particular leadership attributes identified in interviews with key decision-makers included (1) insider status as a "reservation son" born and raised at GSP, (2) an aggressive, in-the-trenches managerial style, and (3) humble and deeply religious character. Though he fired or disciplined hundreds of his staff, he still won respect and led GSP to full compliance. One officer who had been fired by Newsome (and rehired at the Rogers facility) echoed the praise of several of the key decision-makers: "[H]e knows how to get the best out of staff and inmates."

Nearly all key decision-makers described the case as chiefly concerned with "running a constitutional prison." While this generally included the conditions and procedures at GSP, a more specific subset of issues included sanitation, food, safety, overcrowding, medical care, non-discriminatory procedures for solitary confinement, use of force, and impoundment of personal property. Other issues considered important, judging by the response rate of key decision-makers in the focused interviews, included integration (four), federalism (three), and relations between DOR and GSP (two). While four respondents considered racial integration an important goal of *Guthrie*, at least two questioned whether it was ever successful or even appropriate at GSP: "While integration is considered good on the outside [of prison], on the inside it's harmful." Three key decision-makers saw the case as "Georgia versus the Feds," and questioned the state's antagonistic posture when improvements could have been made right away. Some key decision-makers focused this complaint on federal district court intervention in state prisons: "There are some things a court shouldn't even deal with . . . many things ought to be left to the discretion of prison administrators . . . many issues were of less than constitutional level [in *Guthrie*] . . . it got to be ridiculous." Finally, two saw the improvements in communications and relations between DOR and GSP that resulted from the extended lawsuit as an important issue. One subject declared, "*Guthrie* made DOR into one of the best [departments of corrections] in the United States!" Under the scrutiny of the *Guthrie* litigation, key decision-makers noted that the deference traditionally given the GSP warden gave way to a rational, bureaucratic restructuring of prison authority and operations. The increased professionalization of staff and centralization of authority in DOR seemed a key to successful compliance with *Guthrie* consent decrees and stipulations.

When pressed for other, latent issues in *Guthrie*, key decision-makers in the focused interviews shared an interesting list that included remedy-crafting, personality clashes, racial discrimination, judicial activism, federalism, relations between DOR and GSP, limits of the adversarial model, and the stress of litigation/negotiation. Six key decision-makers from the court and plaintiffs' counsel groups indicated that they learned something about remedy crafting, and emphasized that one must design a remedy that will take into account and yet change long-ingrained attitudes and institutional practices.

Another group of six, from defendants, defendants' counsel, and court groups, stressed that the personalities in *Guthrie* told the real story. There were favorite lawyers who did no wrong and got whatever they wanted from the court or other groups (e.g., "[Plaintiffs' counsel] Cullen would get everything in the case."). Some lawyers played the antagonist against whom others fought for honor ("Wage war against Nathan! Nathan told the inmates they were the monitors."). Others were malcontents, always finding some fault, however small, with every reform (e.g., "No matter how good a prison is, prisoners will never be content").

Still other key decision-makers considered racial discrimination the hidden issue behind the case. One subject argued, "[The court] forced a change in GSP [integration] that hasn't yet happened on the streets." Some key decision-makers asserted that the history of segregation and discrimination in Georgia and at GSP caused black inmates to band together during integration, thwarting every effort to relieve racial tensions: "Blacks would band together . . . whites can't band together . . . the Guards didn't care about the violence." One key decision-maker considered *Guthrie* the product of a judge "gone overboard on intervention" and seeking publicity. The need to correct relationships between DOR and GSP was a hidden issue for some. GSP had become too independent of DOR and correctional reform;

Guthrie set GSP in line under DOR guidance. Another issue was the failure of the adversarial model in reforming GSP; "[a]dversarial posture resulted in these ridiculous details." Only when an adversarial posture ended was any progress made in achieving compliance.

The violence at GSP during *Guthrie* struck ten key decision-makers from all groups as a problem related to the case. During the thirteen years' litigation, there was damage to inmate property by inmates and guards, excessive use of force by guards, inmate-on-inmate assaults, and nine homicides. While admitting the lack of stability under *Guthrie*, four of those interviewed argued that the case actually prevented even greater levels of violence. One subject argued with conviction that "[t]he *Guthrie* litigation actually prevented further deterioration and brought hope to the inmates. Inmate violence was a continuation of previous cycles." Six other key decision-makers disagreed, asserting that the destabilizing effect of *Guthrie* on GSP led inmates to believe there was no discipline or safety, so they disrupted ("[There were] eight homicides because the prisoners saw Nathan as their advocate to end run around the warden . . . Nathan *required* no use of physical force by guards"). Those who argued that the case moderated violence at GSP were in the plaintiffs' counsel group and court group. Those who asserted that *Guthrie* heightened violence were drawn from the defendants' counsel, defendants, and court groups.

Nine key decision-makers, spread among the four groups, regarded compliance as problematic and cited evidence to the fact that GSP staff and inmates misunderstood or refused to comply with consent decrees. Key decision-makers declared that *Guthrie* took on a life of its own, commenting,

> [T]he case itself was the problem . . . [it] grew from seven–eight issues to 500–600 separate issues . . . *Guthrie* took on a life of its own . . . court experts came in to expand issues . . . Georgia could have gotten out if it immediately resolved eight–nine issues back in 1973!

As the case grew from 7 issues to over 2,500, measures of compliance were never well defined in the rush to design the remedial decrees. Some members of the defendants' counsel group complained that compliance amounted to fulfilling the desires of plaintiffs, who were never content while imprisoned. Others in this same group argued that compliance difficulties were caused when "legal people" directed prison administrators and prison experts on "how to do it." All, however, agreed that compliance took far too long to achieve.

Other key decision-makers focused on how the problems affected various processes, practices, and relationships. Several emphasized that *Guthrie* placed a tremendous burden on the state budget and on other state prisons ("The number two problem was the financial strain on the State of Georgia"). Several key decision-makers noted the system-wide budget problems caused by *Guthrie* ("The rest of the system was underfunded in order to deal with GSP"). Five members of defendant-state and defendants' counsel groups argued that inmates who were once sent to GSP were shuttled to other state prisons to comply with GSP population limits. Six other members of the defendants, defendants' counsel, and court groups pointed to the impact of *Guthrie* on state spending and argued that *Guthrie* caused the "[d]iverting of funds from other state programs, i.e., education," to cover the costs of renovating GSP. Seven key decision-makers (in all four groups) focused on the administrative problems associated with federal intrusion into DOR and GSP operations. They hypothesized that the extraordinary paperwork and pressure were the major causes of high turnover in key administrators at GSP. The pressure was regarded as so intense that some thought the federal monitor was "out to get DOR." Finally, relations with the media were perceived in both positive and negative terms. Members of the defendant-state and defendants' counsel groups thought they were hurt by negative press coverage and argued that the media did not understand the time involved in compliance. Others in the plaintiffs' counsel and court groups found the media very helpful in persuading state politicians to reform GSP.

An overwhelming majority of the key decision-makers interviewed (78.13 percent) responded that the case solved the problem of unconstitutional conditions and practices at GSP and also resolved issues related to federalism, DOR vs. GSP, and state budgeting. GSP had become a model prison that followed all minimum constitutional standards regarding conditions and practices. The problems caused by *Guthrie* were more varied. They included violence at GSP, lack of compliance, financial strain on the state budget and on other state prisons, federal intrusion (especially by the monitor), job stress at DOR and GSP, and negative media attention. Four key decision-makers perceived no problems caused by the case.

The consensus among key decision-makers that the practices and physical conditions at GSP were transformed by *Guthrie* was enthusiastically expressed. Members of the defendants group boasted that GSP was now one of the best prisons in the country. A member of the court group praised the changes at GSP for "[l]egitimate control of prisoners, the facility, rational classification, environment, professional staff—no single significant issue was not solved!" Even members of the plaintiffs' counsel group commented favorably on "the entire way the prison is [now] run." Six key decision-makers identified yet other improvements in relations between DOR and GSP, the federal and state government, and state budgeting officials, because *Guthrie* "[b]rought the state system to modern penal level." Two members of the defendant-state group believed that GSP finally got what it deserved from the state budget, while one member of the defendants' counsel group was glad to see GSP under state control again. Members of plaintiffs' counsel and defendants groups thought DOR communicated more effectively with GSP.

Most key decision-makers thought the case affected other groups as well as GSP staff and inmates, including other prison systems, the citizens of Reidsville and Tattnall County, and the citizens of Georgia.

Key decision-makers seemed to think of the smaller details in assessing the impact of the *Guthrie* case on prison administration. Although no respondents indicated a sense of some more general impact on prison administration, they remarked on the increased professionalism of GSP staff, the constitutional procedures now practiced at GSP, the state-of-the-art technology and architectural changes at GSP, and improved relations between the federal and state prison authorities, within the Georgia prison system and between DOR and GSP. Finally, some remarked that everything at GSP was affected, arguing that the case grew to include nearly every aspect of GSP.

7

Resources and Remedies in *Guthrie*

This chapter will examine two questions: (1) How did the budget for GSP change in the course of litigation and what were the important factors in that process? and (2) What were the major remedies undertaken and how did settlement patterns change in the course of the litigation?

Budgetary Politics in *Guthrie*

Great interest has developed over the impact of federal court intervention in prisons on state budgets. Early reviews of the law (Comment, 1970) claimed that there were strict constraints on federal judicial authority to direct the expenditure of state funds (i.e., for prison construction). More recent empirical assessments suggest that federal court orders have an effect on state spending for prisons far beyond these limits (Feeley, 1989; Harriman and Straussman, 1983). Furthermore, a survey of agency administrators in eight states indicates that this court intervention is changing the nature of state budgeting decisions (Hale, 1979). However, others argue that courts are merely the catalysts and handy scapegoats for long overdue legislative expenditures on capital improvements in corrections (Moss, 1985; Taggart, 1986, 1989). Do prisoners now have a collective right to certain state expenditures that were once allocated by the democratic process (Straussman, 1986)? While some contend that courts don't care about the costs imposed on state budgets (e.g., Glazer, 1978; Nagel, 1984), others cite evidence of some court awareness and concern for minimizing these burdens (Cooper, 1985, 1988; Yarbrough, 1985). A systematic understanding of institutional reform litigation requires further attention to the interaction of key decision-makers, including judges, in the recognition and accommodation of budgetary realities (Cooper, 1985).

What did *Guthrie* cost? There is no simple answer to this query. At the time of Judge Alaimo's final permanent injunction, the newspapers estimated that over "$100 million worth of changes [were] made" during the fourteen-year litigation (*Florida Times-Union*, 6/27/85; *Atlanta Constitution*, 6/27/85). However, these figures included only the costs of structural changes made at GSP and not attorneys' fees, the fees of court-appointed personnel, and the time and expense to the plaintiffs and defendants. Nor did the figures include the related costs of alternative correctional institutions built to house the inmates diverted by court order from the overcrowded GSP.

Some estimates of costs were available, however, from archival and focused interview data. Appendix F summarizes GSP budgets from fiscal year 1976 through fiscal year 1986. The dollar numbers include both capital and non-capital expenditures at GSP during *Guthrie*, but do not include the final payment of the special monitor's fees in 1982, or the final bill from plaintiffs' counsel (LDF and Georgia Legal Services) from 1979 through 1986. While some budget items were not related to the demands of remedial decrees in *Guthrie* (e.g., $410,000 for a new prison cannery in fiscal year 1978), most capital and non-capital expenditures related in some way to the litigation. In this sense, nearly all expenses at GSP related to *Guthrie*. The aggregate cost, then, to the defendants (and the state of Georgia), exclusive of legal fees, was $249,656,383 over ten fiscal years.

The fees involved in the court litigation of *Guthrie* included court filing fees, transcription and legal stenography fees, plaintiffs' counsel fees, fees of court- and plaintiff-appointed expert witnesses, fees of court-appointed special masters and special monitors, travel expenses incurred by defendants' counsel, and extensive copying costs. The fees of defendants' counsel are not available, since the Georgia attorney general's office did not charge a fee of the defendant-state. However, the total number of involved assistant attorneys general (see appendix E) demonstrates that legal and court costs to the defendant-state were substantial, even if not billed. The plaintiffs' counsel, the Legal Defense Fund, settled for $650,000 in attorney's fees from 1972 to 1979; although they had documented $1,421,209 in expenses and fees through December 1979. Legal fees in the budget summaries

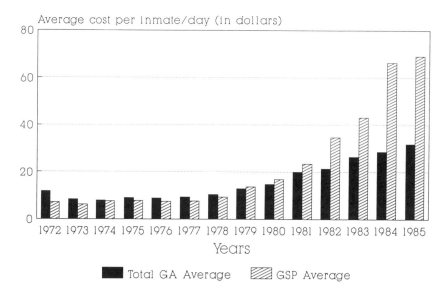

Fig. 1
Georgia State Prison (GSP) and total Georgia average cost per inmate per day

prepared by DOR (see appendix F) total $2,666,061 but do not include
the final payments to the Legal Defense Fund from 1980 to 1985 (est.
$100,000) and Georgia Legal Services Corporation from 1978 to 1986
(est. $3,300,000), or Special Monitor Nathan's fees and expenses in
1982 (est. $600,000). These additional costs may have pushed the
total costs of legal fees, excluding defendants' counsel costs, to over
$6,666,061 for the fiscal years 1976 through 1987.

During this period of litigation the cost to care for inmates at GSP
rose dramatically. This was partly due to the spiraling inflation in the
1970s and early 1980s that affected all Georgia correctional institutions. As outlined in figure 1, the average cost at all Georgia correctional institutions, including GSP, per inmate per day, went from
nearly seven dollars in fiscal year 1972 to over thirty-one dollars by
fiscal year 1985. However, costs at GSP soared past this average rate of
increase. From an average cost per inmate per day of six dollars in
fiscal year 1972 (below the state average), GSP came to average nearly
seventy dollars by fiscal year 1985, or more than double the state
average rate of about thirty-one dollars. The differences in costs may
be attributed to the mandates required by remedial decrees in *Guthrie*
at GSP but not directed at other Georgia correctional institutions.

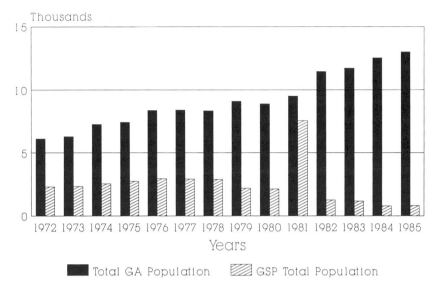

Fig. 2
Georgia State Prison (GSP) and total Georgia inmate population

However, many key decision-makers noted that these mandates were implemented in all other Georgia prisons. DOR officials maintained that all appropriate requirements of conditions and procedures in *Guthrie* were implemented at all facilities, not just GSP.

The dramatic change in cost per inmate at GSP may be due to circumstances peculiar to the maximum security changes at GSP and to general technological changes in prisons. From fiscal year 1972 to fiscal year 1978, GSP was the largest prison in the state and housed the greatest number of inmates (figure 2). There was little attention to security in the structure and design of GSP prior to 1978; the overcrowded open dormitories and fenced yards design were borrowed from facilities for juvenile offenders. Like Mississippi's Parchman Prison, GSP was simply "the farm" for Georgia's convicts of nearly every level of security, including those who were mentally ill or developmentally disabled. GSP was quite literally a farm, with the inmates working in the fields and tending livestock for other correctional centers in the state.

As the violence at GSP became more dramatic in the mid-1970s and as decisions were made to end security problems, GSP showed a drastically reduced average number of inmates, as illustrated in figure 2. By fiscal year 1985, GSP had only 800 inmates with over 1,150 guards. Also, the latest technological devices for maximum security prisons were installed. This required new expertise in operations, but also contributed to a decrease in inmate population. This reduction of inmates, then, accompanied increases in prison personnel and contributed to increased costs at GSP. In addition, the maximum security monitoring devices installed throughout the prison involved new technologies that were expensive to acquire and maintain.

Many of the costs incurred in *Guthrie* were due to years of neglect to the physical structure. There is no record of any capital appropriations made by the Georgia state legislature for GSP from 1938 to fiscal year 1972. There may have been certain unrecorded and small capital funds expended at GSP during those years, but it is unlikely. GSP was traditionally accorded great praise and deference by state legislators, who viewed it as a "free prison," since the revenues raised by GSP farms paid all costs at GSP with an occasional surplus. Like the old gray barns that dot the Georgia countryside, physical facilities at GSP were considered adequate for their use as long as they remained standing. There was no systematic review of conditions for capital improvements. The isolated location of GSP further removed the deteriorating physical conditions from the everyday scrutiny to which other public structures were subject.

Capital budgeting practices changed at GSP during the *Guthrie* litigation. Soon after taking office in 1970, Governor Carter revised state budgeting practices and included a separate capital budget. But the advent of capital budgeting in Georgia did not prompt the physical changes that came to GSP during Carter's administration. Reviews of physical conditions at GSP prompted only minor renovations of the kitchens, bathrooms, and agricultural facilities. No major security renovations were considered. According to key decision-makers, the murder of a correctional officer at GSP in 1978 was the catalyst that prompted Governor Busbee, the state legislature, and others to take capital improvements in security at GSP more seriously "to make sure this never happens again." As others have theorized (e.g., Taggart, 1986), a great bulk of the costs in *Guthrie* were capital improvements designed to remedy the results of decades-long neglect of the physical structures. At least $100,000,000 was expended by the state of Georgia simply to renovate the long-outdated prison structures at GSP.

Did Judge Alaimo cause these budget changes in *Guthrie?* Cases comparable to *Guthrie* imply that judges may have some authority to, in effect, order state funding to reform state institutions by threat of contempt citation or other equitable remedies (e.g., *Newman v. Alabama*, M.D. Ala., 1979). Others strongly imply that judges have the actual power to direct budgetary decisions (Hale, 1979; Harriman and Straussman, 1983). There is a relationship between institutional reform litigation and significant increases in spending for prisons, but can this be attributed to the judge?

Judge Alaimo was responsible for ordering some actions (e.g., racial integration) that involved the expenditure of some state funds. However, he never expressly ordered that state funds be appropriated for any items except court costs and attorneys' fees. All state capital and non-capital expenditures related to *Guthrie* were based on remedial decrees derived from negotiated stipulations of all parties and approved for the case record by the judge. To say, then, that the court ordered these changes is simply to note that Judge Alaimo formally approved the stipulations and consent decrees of both parties. Of course, the state of Georgia balked when ordered to pay over $70,000 in legal fees to the unpopular special monitor, Vincent Nathan (Pollock, 1983). And the state was ordered to pay the plaintiffs' attorneys' fees for Sanford Bishop, the Legal Defense Fund, and Georgia Legal Services. But even these fees were arrived at after negotiated stipulations by all parties. The judge never used his equitable powers to order state funding for items other than these court costs.

The judge in institutional reform litigation is not wholly responsible for the decisions that prompt budget changes. As discussed previously, Judge Alaimo rarely made decisions by himself in *Guthrie.* Almost all decisions were made by attorneys in negotiations where consent decree and stipulations were presented for the judge's approval and insertion in the case record. Other day-to-day decisions requiring court authority were made by appointed masters, a mediator, or the monitor. These consent decrees, stipulations, and interpretations by court-appointed personnel required state funds for their implementation. But Judge Alaimo merely approved what the parties had already agreed to do.

Judge Alaimo did threaten the use of equitable remedies if the defendant-state persisted in doing nothing toward compliance. Furthermore, he did not accept the lack of funds as a defense. However, only one contempt citation was issued, and that was stipulated to by the defendant-state. Even in those areas where the judge threatened punitive equitable remedy, it focused on noncompliance with consent decrees or stipulations by the defendant-state. Thus, judges do not appear to order, or threaten to order, state funding; they seem to enforce what the parties have already agreed to do.

Why did state spending on GSP go up during the *Guthrie* litigation? State funding for GSP did rise during the litigation. Comparing figures 1 and 2, one can see that costs per inmate at GSP skyrocketed at a time when the number of inmates fell dramatically. While budget changes may be partly attributable to inflation, all key decision-makers agreed that the state of Georgia got serious about running a constitutional and more costly maximum security prison. The old dormitories were replaced with single cells throughout the prison, and the staff/inmate ratio was set at better than one to one. These capital expenditures, part of Project 360, were triggered by the shock experienced by state politicians on learning of the gruesome death of a guard. Poor security enabled the inmates to get the guard. Therefore, it seems that the increased cost of building and maintaining a maximum security prison, and not judicial mandate, resulted in the increased funding for GSP.

Judge Alaimo served as a catalyst for budget changes at GSP: first, when he provided an authoritative forum to deny the legitimacy of existing practices and conditions at GSP, and second, when he approved the consent decrees and stipulations of the parties. Sweeping aside the traditional deference to state prison operations, Judge Alaimo provided the opportunity for outsiders to scrutinize and criticize GSP practices and conditions by constitutional standards. Outside attorneys and experts were granted the authority to inspect records, interview inmates and staff, and recommend changes. These individuals proved successful in portraying a vacuum, or lack of legitimacy, in the practices and conditions of GSP, and pressed for widespread institutional reform. The changes at GSP were not mandated by judicial edict, but resulted from the defendant-state's own admissions of fact, consent decrees, and stipulations approved by Judge Alaimo. These self-confessed shortcomings mandated the abrupt increases in budgetary allocations for GSP. Were it not for Judge Alaimo's provision of an authoritative forum or his approval of proposed orders, the state may never have perceived these constitutional violations or found the money to make these reforms. His influence sped up this process. But Judge Alaimo merely served as the catalyst to facilitate and empower others (including the defendant-state) who actually made these decisions after lengthy discovery, negotiation, and consent.

Comparable cases present similar security crises, often accompanied by violence, that resulted in decisions by state officials to build and maintain maximum security prisons. In the early 1980s in New Mexico, several violent riots resulted in the loss of lives and prompted state action. Attempts at prison reform in New Mexico by litigation moved slowly until the riot gripped public attention and stirred state activity. Observers of the New Mexico prison case commented that the judge did not mandate state expenditure. Rather, the state took on the task of building and maintaining a maximum security prison (Taggart, 1986). The relationship of these crises of security and violence to institutional reform litigation remains to be examined in greater detail.

Dimensions of Remedial Litigation in *Guthrie*

While critics point out the misuse and expansion of equity powers by federal district courts (e.g., McDowell, 1984; Nagel, 1984), others present evidence of Supreme Court limits on the issuance, scope, and duration of remedial decrees (Cooper, 1985, 1988; Yarbrough, 1985). However, questions still exist as to federal district court responsiveness to these Supreme Court edicts and the limits of equity. Case studies of legal compliance indicate that perspectives on the extent of compliance relate to one's legal position (i.e., plaintiff, defendant, or court) in the adversarial structure of the litigation (Harris and Spiller, 1976). It is not clear, however, whether this legal position correlates to key decision-maker perspectives on the nature of judicially managed prison reform.

Phillip Cooper argues that assessments by key decision-makers of the nature of the equitable core remedy may correlate to evaluations of the intrusiveness of court activities (1988). For example, with process remedies, such as contempt citations, a court does not appear to intrude into daily prison operations. On the other hand, in specified particular action remedies (e.g., enforcement of extensive remedial decrees by masters), a court appears to take a major and ongoing part in daily prison operations. Further, key decision-maker evaluation of court intrusiveness may also relate to perspectives on the efficacy of negotiated settlement rather than judgment by a court. Participants favoring negotiated settlement view judgment by a court as too intrusive (e.g., Leeke, 1980). Some observers doubt that negotiated settlement is preferable to, or any less intrusive than, judgment by a court (Cooper, 1988; Fiss, 1984). Systematic inquiry into institutional reform litigation requires comparison of key decision-makers' evaluations of judicial intrusion to perspectives on the nature of the equitable core remedy and the efficacy of negotiated settlement rather than judgment by a court.

Some have argued that the intrusion of courts in reforming prison practice and conditions may be blamed for increased prison violence (Engel and Rothman, 1984, p. 105). In their empirical study of the Texas case, Crouch and Marquart (1985, p. 584) conclude:

> [A]lthough court intervention has made Eastham's operations more consistent with constitutional requirements of fairness and due process, the fact remains that life for the inmates and guards at Eastham is far less orderly than it was before. Authority has eroded and the cell blocks and halls are clearly more dangerous. Our observations [and] . . . data . . . suggest that the push toward the bureaucratic-legal order, at least in the first few years after the decree, lessened control to the point that many are increasingly at risk behind the walls.

Others argue that this is nothing new; with change in the prison system of control comes a realignment of power and the increased risk of prison violence. However, these critics argue that one should not adopt a do-nothing strategy in fear of this possible violence, but instead implement reforms with greater attention to the existing prison social order (Ekland-Olson, 1986; Sykes, 1958). In some respects, however, the literature begs the question: can any improvement after court-ordered reform justify increased prison violence and death during implementation?

In legal/remedial aspects, *Guthrie* is truly an exemplary case because so many alternative remedial strategies were incorporated in its fourteen years. Like many prison institutional reform cases, *Guthrie* began as an *in forma pauperis* brief by inmates seeking a class action lawsuit against the state for unconstitutional prison conditions and

practices. And like the vast majority of such cases, *Guthrie* was resolved by the use of equitable remedies such as court-approved consent decrees and stipulations. *Guthrie* included certain alternatives to
civil litigation, including mediation, improved legal assistance to
inmates, and inmate grievance procedures. Judge Alaimo used the
contempt citation once to enforce remedial decrees, and threatened to
use receivership or other punitive measures if compliance was not
achieved quickly. Special masters were appointed, as well as a special
monitor, to assist the judge in overseeing the case.

Unlike many institutional reform cases, however, the decisions in
Guthrie were never appealed to a higher court. Judge Alaimo and
Governor Busbee were reputed to have agreed to settle the case rather
than continue to litigate an appeal. One can only speculate on the deal
between the governor and the judge, but there is some indication that
the arrangement gave the state more input in the formulation of the
remedial decrees in the case. The settlement of the case almost entirely by court-approved consent decrees and stipulations may not
have been possible had the state pursued full civil trial and appeal.
Had the state gone to trial, Judge Alaimo may have ordered changes as
comprehensive as Judge Johnson's in Alabama, without input by state
authorities. Although all key decision-makers agreed that the case
took far too long to settle, all seemed content with the result at GSP. It
may be that Judge Alaimo foresaw that the state would not have made
the long-lasting changes it made had he mandated it all by judicial
order alone. And the judge would not have enjoyed the high esteem
the defendant-state key decision-makers now hold him in.

Although all parties to the *Guthrie* case appeared satisfied with
Judge Alaimo and the results, they were not in agreement during the
process of remedy formulation. As the preceding chronology of
Guthrie outlines, the key decision-makers disputed nearly every aspect of every consent decree and stipulation in lengthy and intense
negotiation sessions. These sessions, extending intermittently from
before 1977 through 1985, sometimes included the special monitor in
addition to counsel for the plaintiffs and defendants. Defendants'
counsel complained that the remedial decrees exceeded minimum
constitutional standards. But the defendant-state stood behind each
provision of every order as its assented word.

Key decision-makers in *Guthrie* were comparatively more accepting of the remedial decrees they had to live with because these orders

were the results of their efforts. Like other prison cases, the remedial decrees in *Guthrie* included specified particular action with a major and ongoing role for the court in daily prison operations (e.g., Special Monitor Nathan), as well as process remedies where the court does not intrude into daily prison operations to achieve compliance (e.g., contempt citation). These remedies were not singularly designed and imposed by Judge Alaimo. Even though most remedial decrees specified particular action (Cooper, 1985) of the defendant-state, neither Judge Alaimo nor the decrees were regarded as activist or intrusive by any of the parties. This is largely a function of consent decrees and stipulations derived from negotiations and approved for the record by Judge Alaimo. The judge did threaten process remedies, or less specific remedies that did not intrude into the day-to-day operations of GSP, but sanctioned the state generally for overall non-compliance. Members of the defendants and defendants' counsel groups found these threatened process remedies most distressing. Cooper (1988) noted that in the cases he studied key decision-makers perceived process remedies as less intrusive and aggravating than specified particular action remedies. However, in *Guthrie* the key decision-makers argued differently, because specified particular action remedies were perceived as less intrusive. Varying perceptions are clearly due to the different roles the parties played in formulating the remedial decrees. In Cooper's (1988) cases, the judges formulated the remedies, and were blamed for activism and intrusion by the defendant-state and for inadequate remedies by the plaintiffs. In *Guthrie*, the parties formulated the remedies and apparently preferred the specificity of specified particular actions to the more general process remedies. While all parties agreed that remedy formulation took too long in *Guthrie*, they did not think that the specific remedial decrees were too intrusive or that the judge was an activist, as in the cases Cooper studied.

This difference in perceptions by key decision-makers in *Guthrie* and these other cases is important. It implies that Judge Alaimo's strategy of working out a deal with Governor Busbee helped to thwart the problems found in other institutional reform litigation. It also suggests that the tensions and loss of legitimacy experienced by courts in other cases may be attributed to the persons and personalities who formulate these remedial decrees, not to the specified or process nature of the remedy itself. In Mississippi, by contrast, key decision-makers for the defendant-state described Judge Keady as activist and intrusive because of the specified particular actions he formulated in *Gates v. Collier*, 349 F. Supp. 881 (N.D. Miss. 1972), while the plaintiffs viewed the actions as inadequate. Furthermore, while modest improvements have been made at Mississippi's Parchman Prison, the wholesale physical and procedural changes of *Guthrie* have not been duplicated, and Mississippi still lacks a constitutional prison. Instead, the court in *Gates* continues to compel implementation of its 1972 remedial decree, litigating its application in a piece-by-piece fashion.

One legal/remedial aspect of *Guthrie* that was perceived as intrusive or activist was the presence of the special monitor. Members of the defendant-state and their counsel thought that Nathan was out to get them and that he was too involved in daily operations at GSP. Nathan often interpreted remedial decrees in ways that offended these participants. For example, in a consent decree the defendants provided for the purchase of a special Afro-American library section when funds permitted. Nathan interpreted this provision to mean that they must/would purchase the library materials immediately. He was especially adamant because they consented to buy the books and more than one fiscal year had elapsed since that consent.

Controversy over Nathan's role may have been a function of personality clashes rather than a result of the nature of the legal remedy. This possibility underscores the importance of personalities, rather than the nature of remedies, in achieving complete compliance in institutional reform litigation. All members of the defendants and defendants' counsel groups, with one exception, emphasized that he/she disliked Monitor Nathan as a person. The clash of Nathan's northern style with southern manners was profound and resulted in numerous confrontations. All members of the defendants and defendants' counsel groups, as well as some of the court group, would have preferred Judge Alaimo to have carried out this function. We can only speculate that these same key decision-makers may have had less regard for Judge Alaimo had Nathan never come on the scene and the judge been forced to do his own dirty work.

Other participants in the case, however, spoke highly of Monitor Nathan, and some remained in contact with him. It may be that the monitor's onerous task of forcing implementation offended the defendants, and that his personality was but one tool used to achieve total compliance. In short, Nathan may have been the gadfly of *Guthrie* who actually helped to achieve compliance by an antagonistic style and equally antagonistic confrontations.

The nature of negotiation and remedial decrees in *Guthrie*, even though the product of consent, upset behavior at GSP. Did this unsettle the institution so much as to cause the nine homicides and other violence at GSP? This case study offers no conclusive answer to the question. Certain members on each side in *Guthrie* agree that the negotiation and implementation process contributed to instability at GSP. The plaintiffs' counsel and some court personnel argued that this was necessary to change the ingrained behavior of GSP staff. Some even argued that this instability moderated the violence that would have existed otherwise (e.g., guard brutality). However, many of the defendants and their counsel argued that the litigation led inmates to believe there was no discipline and that they could disrupt with impunity. Some went so far as to blame the violence on Monitor Nathan's rejoinder to the inmates that they were the monitors.

The general unsettling of prison authority, accompanied by increased violence during institutional reform litigation, is not well documented. In their study of the Texas institutional reform case, Crouch and Marquart (1985; 1989) inferred that court intervention in prisons escalated inmate–inmate and inmate–guard violence. While violence would surely have existed without the federal court intervention in GSP, the argument that an unstable prison authority contributes to its escalation is persuasive in *Guthrie*. The nature of violence at GSP, often between inmates and staff, indicates that the changes brought by the remedial decrees seriously disrupted the ordinary social organization of the prison. GSP staff thought that they could no longer use force against an inmate, even in self-defense, and they rejected all other mandates as unreasonable. On the inmates' part, the more aggressive of their number feared that the remedial decrees were part of a con game engineered by the court and their own counsel. This perception was especially pronounced after the plaintiffs were excluded from negotiations. Inmates protested that they were in the dark on the progress of their case. Instead of accepting the rational judicialization of GSP to protect them, they embraced the right to take matters into their own hands.

8

The Practice of Rights
in Prison Reform

The changes brought about by this 1972–86 litigation are dramatic. GSP is hardly the same institution today as it was in 1972, as both inmates and correctional officers testify. This book has systematically explored the story of this transformation as recorded in archival data and as told by key decision-makers. The story does not feature a political judge mad with power, nor collusion between the defendants and court to force the state to appropriate more state funds to GSP. Instead, it is the story of many diverse pressures and responses that constitute a practice of rights in *Guthrie*. These dimensions of the litigation were not specific to any particular inmate, set of inmates, or occurrence. They simply came together to address the assorted problems of GSP and bring them to some resolution, as the problems were resolved by different sets of key decision-makers over a fourteen-year period.

The Practice of Rights in *Guthrie*

What rights undergirded the *Guthrie* litigation and what does this tell us about institutional reform litigation? *Guthrie* involved adjudication of all civil rights as they apply to inmates in state prisons. The case interpreted and applied a variety of constitutional and statutory rights to GSP, including provisions of the First, Fourth, Fifth, Sixth, Eighth, and Fourteenth amendments of the U.S. Constitution. The lawsuit also concerned the rights of GSP inmates under certain Georgia statutes (e.g., relating to parole), as well as federal statutes on civil procedure (e.g., class action lawsuits by prisoners under 42 U.S.C.

1983). Of course, these rights were said to belong to the plaintiff-inmates in *Guthrie;* the violation and/or exercise of these rights were the focus of adjudication.

Ordinary presentations in available cases and textbooks speak of inmates' rights as principles that can be clearly stated and authoritatively cited in appellate cases (e.g., Palmer, 1985). These principles appear to be universal in their application to all state inmates. Yet other, more critical literature depicts these civil rights as policy statements that are arbitrarily granted to particular inmates in particular prisons by judges or political officials (e.g., Richards, 1977). Thus, inmates at GSP may enjoy certain rights that inmates in Mississippi's Parchman Prison may not enjoy for another decade, or as the relevant political authorities deem it desirable. Relatedly, ideological changes on the Supreme Court may even sweep some of these rights aside with decisions reflecting a get-tough attitude toward convicts. A third theory holds that instead of being idealized universal principles, rights are part of a larger social practice, that is grounded in the context of what actual persons and personalities do (e.g., Flathman, 1976). Thus, while inmates' rights are somewhat different in Georgia than in Mississippi, the notion of inmates' rights is part of long-standing social values that will not disappear on the whim of a particular U.S. Supreme Court or lower court. In this perspective, inmates' rights are neither absolute principles nor policy whims, but short-hand descriptions of basic social values in which individual behavior is constrained by the actual practice of rights and duties.

The perspectives of key decision-makers in *Guthrie* most closely approximate this third theory of rights. First, inmates' rights were never defined a priori or as universally agreed principles. Instead the rights in *Guthrie* grew from an initial complaint listing 7 basic issues to over 2,500 separate issues on specific aspects of the inmates' lives at GSP (e.g., the temperature of various hot food items). Second, these rights were culled from the plaintiffs' counsel in the process of negotiation, not from the concrete violation of specific rights by the defendants. While the original complaint alluded to specific infractions of inmates' rights, the litigation was not limited to or focused on these infractions. Instead, the key decision-makers tried to look at the entire institution in constitutional terms, regardless of whether this involved a complaint of specific violations of rights. Third, the rights enumerated in *Guthrie* were not simply abstracted or deduced from the value statements found in the U.S. Constitution. Rather, each related inductively to a comparison between the facts found elsewhere and at GSP. These facts were gathered by key decision-makers in large part from the experiences of court-appointed experts on proper prison sanitation, diet, security systems, etc. The key decision-makers in *Guthrie* did not authoritatively apply the judicial opinions found in comparable appellate decisions or specific prison remedial decrees from other states. Nor did they agree as to precisely what these facts meant or how they applied to *Guthrie*. Indeed, they never agreed as to what constituted a constitutional prison, and uniformly referred to the dynamic, changing nature of constitutional conditions and practices related to confinement. In the process, certain rights were modified and compromised to reach a more appropriate strategy for the maximum security prison. In the end, however, nearly all key decision-makers agreed that GSP was a maximum security prison that complied minimally with the inmates' constitutional and other rights.

The practice of rights in *Guthrie* illustrates how key decision-makers thought of inmates' rights as a "half-understood, half-hunch" set of behaviors that was not authoritatively directed by policy outcomes or previous judicial opinions. Judge Alaimo did not singularly discover or announce basic constitutional principles to direct the outcome of the case. Neither did he exercise his will to power over participants to shape a policy direction and outcome. Instead, the judge participated with many other key decision-makers who fiercely disputed but ultimately agreed upon specific procedures and conditions for the day-to-day operation of Reidsville. All key decision-makers agreed to specified particular action remedies, with slightly varying interpretations. *Guthrie*, then, was not driven by the substance (principles), nature (specified or process), or authoritative will (policy) embedded in any of its remedial decrees. Rather, the remedial decrees served as a shorthand for the hard-won consent and stipulations negotiated by the parties. The social practice of rights embedded in the persons and personalities of the key decision-makers, more than any other variable, served to drive the litigation to its ultimate resolution.

This doesn't imply that other theories about the nature of rights are irrelevant. It only concludes that the behavior of rights in *Guthrie* was not driven by perceptions of rights as principle or policy. This study of *Guthrie* reveals that practitioners focused their attention on things other than rights as principles to be followed or policies to be obeyed. They focused on the structure and practical physical details of renovating GSP, the state of the art in maximum security prison facilities, and regulations emulating the best of other prison systems. In the final analysis, the remedial decrees as crafted and implemented were justified by their persuasiveness to all parties, who consented to, stipulated to, or approved them. For key decision-makers, these decrees were not justified by their adherence to principles or the will of a policymaker. Instead, the key decision-makers in *Guthrie* developed resolution and closure of the dispute by reference to a practice of maximum security prison operations modeled on successful designs found in other prison systems or advocated for such institutions. In sum, the practice of rights in prison reform litigation consists of a variety of pressures and responses (Munro, 1986), of which the mandates of legal principles or policies are but a small part.

The Pressures of Prison Reform Litigation

Five major pressures dominated the litigation and the effort to improve GSP. These included (1) increased inmate population, (2) fiscal austerity, (3) isolation of the prison and personnel, (4) more assertive inmates, and (5) racial discrimination.

GSP and all other maximum security prisons faced burgeoning populations in the 1970s and 1980s. Although the facilities at GSP were equipped to handle about twelve hundred inmates in the 1970s, nearly three thousand inmates were warehoused there. Pressures related to overcrowding figured in other prison reform litigation— most notably in Alabama, Arkansas, Louisiana, Mississippi, Ohio, Rhode Island, and Texas.

As society becomes disillusioned with rehabilitation and embraces a policy of incapacitation to dispose of criminal convicts (Sherman and Hawkins, 1981), prison populations are likely to continue to soar. In fact, Rich and Barnett predict only a brief respite in the mid-90s, with a steep increase afterward. They warn correctional policymakers that "[u]nless American states de-emphasize imprisonment as a response to criminal acts or unless there is a real and substantial turning away from criminal behavior, to treat prison over-crowding as a transient problem is to run a high risk of falling prey to an illusion" (1985, p. 789).

Fiscal austerity affects prison operations in two directions at the same time: citizens object to rising taxes and prison operations become more costly. As more people are sent to prisons, citizens demand fiscal conservatism, which limits correctional funds. For example, the construction cost of new maximum security prisons is estimated now at $70,000 per cell, and may exceed $300,000 when the financing costs of interest charges on prison bonds are considered (Clear and Cole, 1986, p. 407). Maximum security prisons are also costly to operate at upwards of $20,000 per year per inmate (Fox, 1985, p. 167). Finding state funds to pay these costs may require monies originally intended for education, roads, and more politically popular programs (Weinstein, 1982). While Georgia political authorities found these funds in a time of recession, the effort was protracted and not without political losses. Political authorities in states such as Mississippi and Texas have yet to find funds necessary for institutional reforms and may not be able to pay the political costs if they do.

Location and long-term capital neglect have isolated prison facilities and personnel. Most older facilities, such as GSP, were placed in rural areas under the farm model of maximum security prisons. This model was largely intact in the 1970s in many states, including Alabama, Arkansas, Connecticut, Georgia, Mississippi, New York, and Texas. Although amended or replaced by the prison industry model, as in Ohio (Cooper, 1988), neither the farm nor the industry design was suited for maximum security prisons. Complicating this is the fact that these prisons are far from state capital officials in terms of both location and administration. Prisons in Alabama, Arkansas, Georgia, Mississippi, Texas, and many other states are so isolated geographically that without periodic review by state authorities, they simply did not keep pace with changes in maximum security systems and technology. New personnel were recruited from the isolated, rural towns that developed around these prisons and were not likely to bring new ideas. Until the 1980s, GSP staff were recruited locally, as were staff at rural maximum security prisons in Alabama, Arkansas, Mississippi, and Texas. Although it is possible for some of these staff to have a more cosmopolitan perspective—GSP Warden Newsome was raised on the grounds at Reidsville—it isn't likely.

According to all the key decision-makers in *Guthrie*, inmates adopted a more aggressive posture in the course of the litigation. Certainly in many prisons inmates appear more assertive than they did thirty years ago. Some observers argue that inmates are more rights conscious and invoke these rights more frequently (Jacobs, 1980). Others think that inmates and other oppressed minorities have found rights-talk a valuable source of rhetoric (Williams, 1987). Of course, it is possible that this assertiveness may be a function of the declining use of force in prisons. Nevertheless, inmates are now more vocal and sophisticated in voicing their complaints. The pressures on prison management that resulted from staged protests in Atlanta, walks to Reidsville, and numerous newspaper criticisms of GSP were considered by many key decision-makers as important influences in the case.

Racial discrimination was and will remain an important pressure in prison reform litigation as long as a disproportionate share of inmates is black and Hispanic. Over 60 percent of the inmates at GSP in the 1970s were black, a pattern similar to other state prison systems in Alabama, Mississippi, and Texas. To be sure, racial discrimination is not peculiar to southern prisons, as it also emerges in the Midwest and West (see Cooper, 1988). Complicating this is the recruitment of prison personnel from the rural, isolated communities that have not historically been at the forefront of the civil rights movement.

The Responses to Prison Reform Litigation

All empirical accounts of prison reform litigation document resistance by the defendant-state, even in Arkansas, where corrections officials initially supported litigation as a means to more state funds. The Arkansas officials soon found the lawsuit more of an imposition than a source of additional appropriations and resisted it (Harris and Spiller, 1976). Other major responses to institutional reform litigation include administrative reorganization, litigation and appeal, and mediation and/or negotiation. The Guthrie case may be unique, as each response was tried out and none worked.

Resistance to institutional reform litigation by the defendant-state centered on access to information about prison practices. Patterns are more overt in litigation, more covert in mediation/negotiation. Obviously, if plaintiffs' counsel or the courts could obtain all the information the remedies required, the defendants' liability or noncompliance would be easily ascertained. Defendants in Texas have consistently tried to control information by limiting inmate access to lawyers and law libraries. Additionally, they have tried to remove or at least hassle inmate counsel (DiIulio, 1987; Martin and Ekland-Olson, 1987). Similar attempts were documented in *Guthrie*, as well as in Arkansas, Alabama, Mississippi, and Ohio litigation. Such resistance is by nature a temporary strategy, albeit protracted, that is usually brought to a close by the imposition (or threat) of severe, punitive judicial remedies such as contempt of court.

Administrative reorganization of authority and personnel within a prison, between prisons, and between prisons and state correction departments occurs in most, if not all, prison reform cases. Typically initiated by the top executive authority in the state corrections department or by the governor, efforts are made to centralize responsibility and to control potentially liable practices. New structures of authority within GSP were designed by wardens Montgomery, Austin, and Newsome to control staff behavior and to limit excessive use of force. GSP developed new relations with other state prisons as inmates were diverted to institutions to relieve overcrowding and to comply with court orders at GSP. Finally, DOR developed direct authority over and sustained communications with the GSP warden. DOR Commissioner Evans supported the GSP warden and eliminated the more autonomous practices whereby GSP wardens had a private line to the Georgia state legislature. The *Guthrie* case opened up GSP operations to state capital officials and brought the maximum security prison under DOR's control.

Similar patterns occurred in *Ruiz v. Estelle*, where the Texas Department of Corrections (TDC) was forced to submit to the authority of the governor. TDC commissioners such as George Beto had built up a fiefdom with offices away from the state capital, little communication with state offices, and "big farm" prison profitmaking. Judge Justice's work in the *Ruiz* case helped to end the TDC strangle hold on information and authority and to bring Texas corrections back to the capital (DiIulio, 1987; Martin and Ekland-Olson, 1987). Similarly, others have documented administrative reorganization of corrections in Alabama, Arkansas, Louisiana, Mississippi, Ohio, and Rhode Island (Cooke and Panko, 1986; Cooper, 1988; Harris and Spiller, 1976; Hawkes, 1985; Yarbrough, 1981).

Litigation and appeal through pleadings, pre-trial discovery, trial, and appellate proceedings are found in all prison reform lawsuits. *Guthrie* involved substantial pleadings and pre-trial discovery litigation, although the case never went to trial or involved an appeal. The case, however, was fiercely litigated by opposing teams of attorneys determined to take the case all the way to the Supreme Court. In contrast, the Texas prison reform lawsuit has involved far more lengthy and hostile litigious efforts in trial and appeal (Crouch and Marquart, 1990). Litigation in Mississippi's *Gates v. Collier* was shorter, spanning the pleading, pre-trial discovery, and trial steps in only seven months (Cooke and Panko, 1986), while South Carolina's limited attempts at litigation through pleadings and pre-trial discovery (avoiding trial and appeal) paralleled *Guthrie* (Leeke, 1980).

At first glance, litigation appears to be the fastest and least costly means of dispute resolution. A relatively small set of attorneys present all issues to a judge who designs a remedial decree in quick fashion. Ordinary civil litigation, then, does seem less costly, more speedy, and more satisfactory to clients than mediation, arbitration, and other alternatives (Trubeck et al., 1987). But institutional reform litigation begins at the close of trial. Unlike ordinary civil litigation, institutional reform cases are characterized by extensive appeals that delay reforms (e.g., Cooper, 1988). Furthermore, implementation is considerably more difficult than ordinary civil remedies (i.e., compensatory damages). Prison reform cases in Mississippi and Alabama that were resolved by trial still featured judge-crafted remedial decrees to be implemented over long periods of time (Cooke and Panko, 1986; Yarbrough, 1984). For example, judges in Mississippi have yet to see extensive changes at Parchman Prison, where litigation has occurred in a piecemeal fashion (Cooke and Panko, 1986). Judge Johnson in Alabama observed that every time he decided a prison reform case, it came back to him in a newly designed class action lawsuit. Finally, he sidestepped trial litigation and pushed the parties to a consent agreement that he monitored successfully with an implementation committee (Yarbrough, 1984).

Mediation or negotiation is attempted, to different degrees, in all the prison reform lawsuits analyzed in the literature. However, only two big prison cases (South Carolina and Georgia) successfully used mediation and/or negotiation to achieve ultimate settlement and compliance. In the South Carolina case, *Mattison v. South Carolina Board*

of Corrections, No. 76–318 (D.C. S.C. 1976), the then commissioner
of corrections (Leeke) argued that litigation to trial with judicially
crafted remedies was too intrusive, so a settlement was negotiated. In
two years, the defendant-state and plaintiff-inmates reached settlement on all issues, with complete implementation the following year
(Leeke, 1980). To be sure, the *Guthrie* case involved literally thousands of issues not even considered in the South Carolina case. This
contributed to mediation and negotiation that ran from 1973 through
1985. The resolution in both the South Carolina and Georgia cases,
however, appeared more satisfactory to all parties than the cases with
trial, appeal, and judicially crafted remedies (for other comparison
see Cooper, 1988). Witness, for example, that years after trial, the
judges who originally tried and decided cases in Texas, Arkansas,
and Mississippi are still being blamed for an excessive imposition of
judicial will.

Conclusion

While many efforts to study institutional reform litigation have been
pathological, this study has focused on a lawsuit that worked to
achieve the desired change. The pathological perspective of other
research has focused attention on the failures of courts in institutional
reform litigation and typically concludes with a recommendation that
courts defer to other political officials. How, though, can courts turn
away from a blatant disregard of human dignity in institutions that
have deteriorated due to political neglect? Judge Alaimo, like Judge
Johnson in Alabama, felt compelled to respond. And, as we have
seen, their involvement has not necessarily featured an imperial judiciary imposing its will on others. GSP was transformed by negotiated
consent decrees and stipulations, not by judicial mandate. The rela-
tive success of this approach suggests that these and other institutions
may be reformed more permanently by this approach. The judge need
not personally undertake day-to-day implementation to transform an
institution. *Guthrie* attests to the success of a strategy, albeit protracted, of hard-bargained consent and stipulation of the parties without judicial fiat. To be sure, Judge Alaimo put pressures on the defendants' and plaintiffs' counsel to achieve these consent decrees and
stipulations, but he did not design or implement them.

At what costs? Why should the state spend a disproportionate share of its scarce financial resources on convicts—the least deserving? In litigating *Guthrie*, was the excessive loss of life justifiable? Not only was there a tremendous burnout rate and turnover among counsel and the parties, but there was more traumatic suffering at GSP, where guards and inmates were murdered. Empirical studies of violence during institutional reform litigation at the Texas prisons concluded, "[The] push toward the bureaucratic-legal order . . . lessened control to the point that many are increasingly at risk behind the walls" (Crouch and Marquart, 1985, p. 584).

Litigating prison reform is filled with frustration for all involved. Prison violence appears to proliferate. Compliance seems elusive. Costs mount far beyond the original estimates. Changes seem to come all too slowly. More and more inmates pour into the prison system. Yet the continuing and increasing reliance on incarceration by society results in the construction of new prisons for yet another era of prison reform. Although extreme prison violence and abuses were roundly condemned by the press and public, the practice of caging criminals is never seriously challenged. The accounts of key decision-makers in all the prison cases share this common sense of frustration. Given all the problems, one has to ask: For what good purpose is all this litigation?

Twenty years ago the courts avoided these cases and the frustrations that accompany the systematic reform of a prison or prison system. *Guthrie* and other prison cases illustrate the practical fashion by which a court can keep trying until a way is found to implement constitutional standards. The failure of any particular means toward that end does not condemn the entire effort. The struggle toward constitutional prisons is not over until every feasible plan has been tried.

Guthrie and other prison cases also demonstrate that prison litigation can help accomplish this change. The inhuman practices and conditions at GSP that the special monitor described in 1979 no longer exist. The reign of terror against inmates has ended. Today, guards do not routinely beat, mace, and shoot inmates. Inmates and guards no longer die from a lack of safety and protection. Guards can walk the cells without having to carry illegal knives and pickax handles to protect themselves. The medical, mental, nutritional, educational, and recreational needs of inmates are now provided for. GSP is a clean prison; on his final inspection of the prison, Judge Alaimo remarked that "you could eat off the floor." Inmates are humanely cared for and most have a practical opportunity to rehabilitate. Those changes were the result, in large part if not solely, of the *Guthrie* litigation.

Appendix A
Methodology

The sources of evidence used in this case study are outlined below and listed in appendix B. Of the six basic sources of evidence for case study research outlined by Yin (1984, pp. 79–89), five were used in this analysis. These included (1) archival records, (2) other documents, (3) interviews, (4) direct observations, and (5) physical artifacts. All sources consisted of quantitative as well as qualitative evidence.

The archival records consisted of court records, transcripts, organizational records, service records, maps/charts or physical resources, agency survey data, and some personal records from calendars. Most archival records were received on loan from the Georgia attorney general's office. This loan included four legal filing cabinets filled with a complete set of court records, transcripts, organizational records, and some personal records. Some archival records were also given by plaintiffs' counsel Bob Cullen and by Judge Alaimo.

Other documents included news clippings, letters, agendas, meeting minutes, and internally used documents and reports. Many documents were incorporated in the files loaned by the Georgia attorney general's office, including numerous letters, news clippings, meeting minutes, and internal documents/reports. Other documents were gathered with the assistance of special librarians of the Georgia Room at the University of Georgia main library. These documents included a complete set of news clippings on GSP from state and national papers, primary historical sources on the development of GSP since 1933, and the personal papers of state politicians who were involved in the *Guthrie* litigation.

All key decision-makers in the *Guthrie* litigation were sought for focused interviews: a set of carefully worded questions posed in open conversation over a period from one to three hours. The criteria for selecting key decision-makers, the questions asked, and the subjects' names and positions are as follows.

From a study of archival records and documents, it appeared that some authorities were far more extensively involved in the litigation than others at any given time. For example, while many in the Georgia attorney general's office signed court documents, only certain assistant attorneys general were designated for all correspondence and made all court appearances. This list of potential key decision-makers was checked against the advice of external authorities, including other researchers, the dissertation committee, and key decision-makers themselves during interviews.

After archival and document analysis, a list of carefully worded questions for focused interviews with key decision-makers was designed. These questions focused on litigation roles, issues, problems, and impact. The questions included:

ROLES   What was your part in the case?
               What individuals/groups were influential in directing the outcome of the case?
               Is there any individual who stands out in the development of the case (e.g., judge, attorneys, warden, monitor)?
               What effect did he/she have?
               (If critical): How could it have been improved?

ISSUES   What are the important issues raised by the case?
               Do you think the case raises any other issues or problems we haven't mentioned?

PROBLEMS   What problems were created by the case?
               What problems did the case help to solve?

IMPACT   Who/what was affected by this case?
               How did the case affect prison administration, particularly and generally?

Thirty-seven key decision-makers were identified by this method. Of these, thirty-four were interviewed with the aforementioned focused interview instrument. Included were plaintiffs' counsel, defendants' counsel, defendants, and those associated with the court. Beyond this list of key decision-makers, three GSP inmates and five GSP correctional officers were interviewed in open-ended conversational fashion. The names, positions, and dates of those interviewed are listed in appendix B.

Direct observation required field visits to a site. This case study involved direct observation of the final injunctive hearing at the GSP hearing room, Reidsville, Georgia, on June 26, 1985.

Physical artifacts consisted of physical evidence of the case (e.g., buildings, rooms, conditions of the prison). Tours of GSP facilities, including the Rogers Correctional Institution, were conducted over a two-day period (June 26 and 27, 1986). Additionally, site visits were made to Judge Alaimo's courtroom in New Brunswick, Georgia, offices of plaintiffs' and defendants' counsel, the defendants' offices, and the negotiation suite at the Hilton Inn on Jekyll Island, Georgia.

Appendix B

Sources of Evidence

This appendix contains a complete list of the sources used in conducting this case study of *Guthrie*. The sources are listed in order and include categories of archival records, documents, interviews, direct observations, and physical artifacts.

Archival Records. This source of evidence includes items found in the official court records of the *Guthrie* case. Because a complete list of every document would be too lengthy for this appendix, only the concluding court actions are summarized: orders, stipulations, consent decrees, or reports. Not summarized, but important to a complete understanding of *Guthrie*, are the letters, briefs, complaints, answers, motions, hearing transcripts, and procedural records, and the defendants' organizational, service, architectural, survey, and miscellaneous records leading up to these concluding court actions.

1.1. Order, 4/10/74: racial desegregation of GSP.

1.2. Hearings Transcripts (11 volumes), 6/76–7/76: to determine whether correctional officers were using excessive force against inmates and intimidating inmates from testifying at hearings.

1.3. Phase I Hearings Transcripts (10 volumes), 11/11/76–11/24/76: to take testimony from experts concerning medical, penological, psychiatric, and environmental conditions at GSP.

1.4. Order, 11/26/76: protecting inmates during hearings by Special Master Pipkin and concerning inmate assaults, corporal punishment, plaintiffs' counsel's access to prison.

1.5. Phase II Hearings Transcripts (40 volumes), 3/28/77–7/8/77: concerning all aspects of GSP (conditions and practices); included the testimony of over 180 witnesses and more than 100 exhibits.

1.6. Temporary Order, 7/3/79: temporary segregation of GSP dormitories through a checkerboard pattern, due to the violence of March, June, and July.

1.7. Consent Decree & Order, 7/19/78: creation of a law library, inmate access to law library materials, and increased access to the courts through Prisoner Legal Counseling Project administered by the University of Georgia School of Law at GSP.

1.8. Consent Decree & Order, 8/4/78: covered every major issue raised in the 1973 *Guthrie* amended complaint and more, including overcrowding, racial discrimination, improper use of force, food, discipline, administrative segregation, mail, visitation, publications/reading, religious liberties of Muslim inmates, classification procedures, inmate housing and hospital job assignments, fire prevention, and inmate grievance procedures.

1.9. Consent Decree & Order, 12/1/78: extensive stipulations, but less comprehensive than the 8/4/78 Consent Decree, including inmates' personal property, library services, pork-free diet, prison overcrowding, security renovation, hiring of personnel, and vocational, academic, and rehabilitative programs.

1.10. Order, 12/12/78: extended the checkerboard housing order of 7/3/78 but ordered all aspects of GSP to be integrated sometime in the future.

1.11. Order, 12/19/78: defendants must file a plan for GSP integration.

1.12. Plan, 1/15/79: defendants plan to reintegrate GSP by 3/1/79.

1.13. Report, 2/13/79: GSP was reintegrated in one day without any incident.

1.14. Order, 4/12/79: the U.S. Department of Justice Civil Rights Division is appointed as *amicus curiae* to monitor defendants' compliance with consent decrees and court orders.

1.15. Order of Reference, 6/1/79: the court appointed Ohio attorney Vincent Nathan as the special monitor in *Guthrie.* The defendants objected to the unlimited control given Nathan in the original order of reference and on 6/20/79 a new order of reference was issued limiting the scope of the special monitor's authority.

1.16. Findings of Fact, Conclusions of Law, and Recommendations, 10/8/79: Special Master Marvin Pipkin filed his final report generated by the hearings in *Guthrie.* Pipkin recommended that the court retain jurisdiction, refrain from issuing its own remedial decrees, push for stipulations and consent decrees, and use the special monitor to achieve compliance.

1.17. Report, 11/20/79: Special Monitor Nathan's first report on the defendants' state of compliance. Out of thirty areas monitored, nine were in compliance, one wasn't reported, and twenty were in noncompliance.

1.18. Order, 1/7/80: the court's immediate response to the special monitor's first report enjoined GSP from using restricted diets, and directed improvements in administrative segregation and disciplinary isolation units.

1.19. Stipulation, 1/18/80: the parties agreed to allow defendants more time to request over $741,000 from the state legislature to change the administrative segregation and isolation units.

1.20. Order, 2/11/80: confirms Nathan's first report. The monitor's powers are increased to allow supervision of coordination of future compliance efforts by the defendants.

1.21. Stipulation & Order, 2/25/80: defendants agreed to submit plans for administrative segregation and disciplinary isolation units, as well as to the continuation of Special Monitor Nathan.

1.22. Report, 10/26/80: Special Monitor Nathan's second report on the defendants' state of compliance in Building 2, to be replaced by the Rogers Correctional Institution as a part of Project 360. Nathan recommended certain temporary renovations until the building was replaced.

1.23. Stipulation & Order, 12/19/80: approving Nathan's second report.

1.24. Report, 12/31/80: Special Monitor Nathan's third report on the defendants' state of compliance: finds a lack of compliance, but GSP achieving "genuine and continuing cooperation" with DOR. Nathan was optimistic that a framework for compliance had been attained.

1.25. Memorandum & Order, 2/13/81: confirming Nathan's third report.

1.26. Memorandum & Order, 3/16/81: timetable for remedying inadequacies specified in the monitor's third report.

1.27. Stipulation & Order, 3/25/81: defendants adopted policy statements and standards/limitations for the protection of inmates' personal property.

1.28. Order & Stipulation, 3/25/81: adopting disciplinary policies and procedures (later superseded by stipulation & order, 1/2/84).

1.29. Order, Stipulation & Policy Statement, 4/15/81: regarding security/custody classification (later superseded by stipulation, 5/18/83, and policy statement, 5/26/83).

1.30. Memorandum & Order, 4/16/81: rescinding racial balance requirement, implementing classification, disciplinary, and security policies. Also, defendants ordered to expedite single cell construction.

1.31. Order, Stipulation & Report of Special Task Force, 5/11/81: redistribution of Building M inmates (later superseded by Security Custody Classification Plan).

1.32. Stipulation, 5/12/81: regarding inmate possession of weapons (later superseded by Disciplinary Policy).

1.33. Order, 6/1/81: Special Monitor Nathan's recommendations and compliance plan regarding inclement weather plan for Building H.

1.34. Order & Stipulation, 7/17/81: regarding grievance procedure.

1.35. Order, 7/29/81: retaining jurisdiction three more years.

1.36. Order, Stipulation & Agreement of the Parties, 8/31/81: regarding industrial health and safety.

1.37. Order, Stipulation & Agreement, 8/31/81: regarding environmental health conditions and practices.

1.38. Report, 11/2/81: Special Monitor Nathan's fourth report on the defendant's state of compliance: minimal compliance in the twenty-eight major areas. Nathan was optimistic that full compliance would be achieved: "Commissioner Evans and Warden Montgomery have set a course of action that is calculated to achieve substantial compliance with all of the Court's orders in this case in the relatively near future."

1.39. Order, 11/13/81: enforcement of 8/4/78 order on disciplinary convictions incurred between 8/4/78 and 4/20/81, with notice to plaintiff class.

1.40. Order & Stipulation, 12/31/81: approving stipulation by defendants resolving the plaintiffs' motion for show cause and contempt order.

1.41. Order, 1/15/82: confirms Nathan's fourth report.

1.42. Order, 2/18/82: the court ordered Building M closed because of deteriorating conditions.

1.43. Order, 2/18/82: the court required new practices regarding inmates' special leave, medical examinations, and security.

1.44. Order & Stipulation, 3/18/82: revised grievance procedure policy.

1.45. Stipulation & Order, 4/12/82: revised security/custody classification system.

1.46. Stipulation & Order, 4/12/82: revised disciplinary policy and procedures.

1.47. Stipulation, 4/20/82: regarding sanitation, fire prevention, and industrial health and safety.

1.48. Report, 5/12/82: Special Monitor Nathan's fifth report on the defendants' state of compliance, with Samuel V. Hoover, expert on sanitation. Nathan's report relies on a comprehensive audit document (prepared by Nathan). Nathan found the defendants unhelpful and misleading during the audit process.

1.49. Order, 7/2/82: approving defendants' stipulation of 4/20/82 on sanitation, fire safety, industrial health and safety.

1.50. Order, 7/14/82: confirms Nathan's and Hoover's fifth report and gives specific time limits on compliance with all areas, published in *GSP News.* Judge Alaimo promises that if the monitor's sixth report indicates substantial compliance, he will issue a final injunctive order. Otherwise, punitive coercive measures would be imposed.

1.51. Order & Stipulation, 8/23/82: memoranda of interpretation regarding grievance procedures to be printed in *GSP News.*

1.52. Stipulation, 9/10/82: inmate correspondence and inspection of mail.

1.53. Stipulation, 9/23/82: use of strip cells and temporary confiscation of personal property.

1.54. Class Notice Order, 10/6/82: publishing for all inmates at GSP the tentatively approved "Stipulations and Policy Statements," 9/10/82 and 9/23/82.

1.55. Order & Stipulations, 10/6/82: (1) excessive use of force, excessive use of restraints, and misuse of strip cells, and (2) use of force.

1.56. Order, 10/14/82: interpretation of library services, referring back to consent order on library and access to courts, 7/19/78.

1.57. Stipulation, 10/14/82: establishment of a special control unit.

1.58. Order, 11/12/82: approving audit document designed for measuring defendants' state of compliance in all areas.

1.59. Order, 11/29/82: approves amendment to stipulation on inmate correspondence and inspection of mail (stipulation, 9/10/82).

1.60. Order, 12/15/82: confirms Nathan's supplemental report on the elimination of surgical backlog and orders that the mental health plan be implemented. Also approves a stipulation based on defendants' submissions to comply with previous order (7/14/82), restoration of lost earned time, and an incentive plan.

1.61. Order, 12/29/82: confirms Nathan's special report on the inmate grievance procedure from investigations of defendants' stipulated use of force, excessive use of restraints, and misuse of strip cells.

1.62. Order, 3/18/83: approves stipulations on protective custody, special control unit, use of force, library services, strip cells, mail, and temporary confiscation of personal property.

1.63. Order, 4/21/83: protective order enjoining retaliation against inmates participating in the litigation.

1.64. Order, 4/21/83: order governing changes by the warden in prison operation covered by the *Guthrie* orders.

1.65. Order & Stipulation, 4/21/83: modifying policy statement on administrative segregation.

1.66. Stipulation, 4/28/83: mental health and mental retardation plan.

1.67. Order, 5/6/83: approving stipulation to modify special control unit policy statement.

1.68. Order, 5/13/83: approves stipulation (4/28/83) on mental health and mental retardation plan.

1.69. Order, 5/16/83: memorandum of understanding including grievance procedure.

1.70. Order, 5/16/83: approves the incentive plan on an interim basis.

1.71. Order, 5/19/83: confirms Nathan's fifth report and all supplements, and continues the monitorship.

1.72. Joint Motion to Modify Class Definition, 5/27/83: opens the class of plaintiff-inmates to include all inmates at GSP (white and black) since the class action was certified in 1974, except those expressly waiving their participation.

1.73. Order, 6/1/83: temporarily approving stipulation agreements and plans on correspondence and mail inspection; vocation, academic, and rehabilitation services; Prisoner Legal Counseling Project; elimination of lifers club; security staffing and procedures; special control unit; and the mental health/mental retardation plan.

1.74. Consolidated Class Notice Order, 6/16/83: to inmates on the above matters along with admissions and orientation procedures, incentive plan, temporary use of handcuffs on inmates in Building M, and three orders from 4/21/83 (protection of inmates, administrative detention, and modification of orders).

1.75. Order, 6/16/83: approves the audit documents revised on 5/4/83.

1.76. Order, 6/27/83: confirms certain audit items (FT-2, FT-6, FT-7).

1.77. Order, 6/29/83: modifies class definition.

1.78. Stipulation on Personal Property, 7/27/83: reimbursement for lost personal property.

1.79. Stipulation on Muslim Rights, 8/17/83: First Amendment rights.

1.80. Stipulation, 8/17/83: a new inmate disciplinary appeals process and grievance procedure.

1.81. Order, 9/7/83: disciplinary policy 590.1.

1.82. Order, 10/7/83: clarifies class definition given in 6/29/83 order and confirms stipulations on Muslim rights, new disciplinary appeal and grievance procedures, and reimbursement of lost personal property.

1.83. Order, 10/7/83: Judge Alaimo confirms all 1983 stipulations and orders.

1.84. Report, 12/1/83: Monitor Nathan's sixth report on the defendants' state of compliance. Defendants are found in noncompliance in most areas and Nathan recommends punitive measures be taken by the court. Once again, Nathan finds the defendants unhelpful (unreliable self-audit by defendants). Use of several experts: Hoover, Markel, Hulla, King, Hirshorn, and Harness.

1.85. Order, 12/6/83: terminates Nathan's monitorship, addresses Nathan's sixth report, and sets out a procedure to address ongoing problems in *Guthrie*.

1.86. Stipulation & Order, 1/8/84: on disciplinary policies and procedures relating to the use of strip cells.

1.87. Report, 5/15/85: independent monitor Charles Bell finds minimal compliance in the new Rogers facility (replacing Building 2).

1.88. Order, 6/26/85: Judge Alaimo finds substantial compliance and issues a final injunctive order, no longer retaining jurisdiction over the case. However, he warns that if any orders are violated, he will not hesitate to return.

Documents. This source of evidence includes news clippings, personal letters, agendas, meeting minutes, and internally used documents and reports. For the purpose of this appendix, these documents are summarized under two subtopics: News Clippings and Other Documents.

2.1. *News Clippings* from local, state, and national newspapers and magazines were incorporated in the files loaned by the Georgia attorney general's office. Many other news clippings on GSP and the *Guthrie* case were obtained from the Georgia Room at the University of Georgia main library.

2.1.1. "Report of Mr. A. C. Stone, Chairman of Committee on Penitentiary," *Atlanta Constitution* (1899).

2.1.2. Eugene V. Debs, "Behind Prison Walls" (pamphlet on the Atlanta Penitentiary and Georgia prisons, July 1922).

2.1.3. "Our Georgia Jails," *Thomasville Daily Times-Enterprise* (1/23/24).

2.1.4. "Tattnall County Prison Completed," *Atlanta Journal* (1/10/37).

2.1.5. E. D. Rivers, "Prison Reform In Georgia," *The Atlantian* 1 (July/August 1938): 4–5, 21.

2.1.6. "Tattnall State Prison Stresses Rehabilitation," *Atlanta Constitution* (1/29/51).

2.1.7. "Some of Georgia's Convicts Now Sleep In Marble Halls," *Augusta Chronicle* (8/30/51).

2.1.8. "Serious Problem Cited In State Prison System," *Atlanta Journal* (11/24/54).

2.1.9. "Georgia's 'Piney Woods Alcatraz' Self-Sufficient Prison Community," *Lyons Progress* (11/24/55).

2.1.10. "Fair Play Runs Prison," *Atlanta Journal* (3/22/57).

2.1.11. "They Rehabilitate Land and Prisoners at Reidsville," *Atlanta Journal & Constitution Magazine* (3/15/59).

2.1.12. "Reidsville Inmates Ask Help," *Augusta Chronicle* (10/28/60).

2.1.13. "Georgia Prison Cruelty: The Dread 'Hole' In the News Again," *Atlanta Journal & Constitution* (10/21/62).

2.1.14. "Warden Never Witnessed Any of 116 Electrocutions," *Atlanta Journal* (5/24/63).

2.1.15. "Sanders Junks Old State Prison Plans," *Augusta Herald* (6/21/63).

2.1.16. O. P. Hanes, "Georgia Prison Reform Took 30 Years," *Atlanta Journal* (6/28/63).

2.1.17. "Patrolmen Were Ready For Action: 35 Injured At Reidsville," *Augusta Chronicle* (9/4/63).

2.1.18. "Corrections Unit Sued by Prisoner," *Atlanta Journal* (1/8/64).

2.1.19. "Dutton To Become Warden," *Atlanta Constitution* (12/10/65).

2.1.20. "Escape Tunnel Found at Reidsville Prison," *Macon Telegraph & News* (11/29/66).

2.1.21. "State Prison Population Drops 1,800 Since 1961," *Atlanta Constitution* (12/28/66).

2.1.22. "Roof Top Escape Route Discovered at Reidsville," *Macon Telegraph & News* (3/14/67).

2.1.23. "Reidsville New Head Has Disciplinary Woes," *Augusta Chronicle* (5/17/67).

2.1.24. "Dr. Arrendale Denies Donated Blood Sale," *Gainesville News* (6/26/67).

2.1.25. "Maddox Blames Prisoners," *Athens Banner-Herald* (2/19/68).

2.1.26. "Desegregation of Prisons Ordered By Federal Courts," *Athens Banner-Herald* (6/28/68).

2.1.27. "Maddox Decries Ruling On Prison Desegregation," *Gainesville Daily Times* (6/28/68).

2.1.28. "High Court Backs Prison Integration," *Atlanta Constitution* (12/17/68).

2.1.29. "Maddox Asks Funds to End Work Camps," *Macon Telegraph & News* (1/7/69).

2.1.30. "Reidsville Prison Revamp Planned by New Warden," *Atlanta Journal* (4/1/70).

2.1.31. "New Prison Chief Talks About Criminal Justice," *Atlanta Journal & Constitution* (3/21/71).

2.1.32. "Reidsville Grant Aims at Relieving Crowded Conditions," *Augusta Chronicle* (8/28/71).

2.1.33. "Georgia State Prison Trying to Shake Image," *Athens Banner-Herald* (11/9/71).

2.1.34. "State Prison Blasted For Breeding Violence," *Atlanta Constitution* (11/30/71).

2.1.35. "Prisons In Trouble: With Too Little Money, Too Little Space, Georgia's Cells Fester With Problems," *Atlanta Journal & Constitution* (10/12/75).

2.1.36. "Evans Named to Succeed Ault as Penal Director: Experience Factor Cited," *Atlanta Constitution* (11/10/76).

2.1.37. "Overcrowding: Pressing Prison Problem," *Atlanta Constitution* (11/29/76).

2.1.38. "Busbee: Integration Fuels Prison Violence," *Atlanta Constitution* (4/1/78).

2.1.39. "Warden Abolishes Reidsville Committee," *Atlanta Constitution* (5/4/78).

2.1.40. "Inmates Transferred, Resegregated," *Savannah Morning News* (7/15/78).

2.1.41. "Guard, Inmate Killed In Reidsville Riot," *Atlanta Constitution* (7/24/78).

2.1.42. "Reidsville Attack Kills 1, Injures 3," *Atlanta Journal* (8/16/78).

2.1.43. "Racial Separation At Reidsville Extended 30 Days," *Atlanta Journal* (9/1/78).

2.1.44. "Eight Quit In Prison Crackdown," *Atlanta Constitution* (9/15/78).

2.1.45. "ACLU Assails Busbee: Remarks on Prison Slaying Called Unfair," *Atlanta Constitution* (11/7/78).

2.1.46. "Reidsville Prison Begins Dormitory Integration Again," *Atlanta Journal* (2/3/79).

2.1.47. "Prison Medical Center to Increase Care," *Augusta Chronicle* (8/2/79).

2.1.48. "Prison Protest: 100 Marchers Leave Savannah On Trek to Reidsville," *Atlanta Constitution* (8/7/79).

2.1.49. "Reidsville Protester Drowns During March," *Atlanta Journal* (8/9/79).

2.1.50. "Protesters On Hunger Strike," *Atlanta Journal* (8/13/79).

2.1.51. "Guards At Reidsville Brutal, Court Told," *Atlanta Constitution* (12/3/79).

2.1.52. "Monitor Gets New Powers At Reidsville," *Atlanta Constitution* (2/12/80).

2.1.53. "Reidsville Warden Balkcom Dismissed," *Atlanta Constitution* (2/15/80).

2.1.54. "Georgia Prison Official Resigns to Protest Day of Executioner," *Atlanta Constitution* (2/22/80).

2.1.55. "Reidsville Residents Resent New Regime Changes At Prison," *Atlanta Journal* (3/24/80).

2.1.56. "Reidsville: Sentenced To Neglect," *Atlanta Constitution* (4/15/80).

2.1.57. "Sentenced: To Poor Medical Care," *Atlanta Constitution* (4/16/80).

2.1.58. "Monitor, Judge Use Federal Whip to Spur Prison Reform," *Atlanta Constitution* (4/17/80).

2.1.59. "Reidsville's Death Row Will Be Closed By End of August," *Atlanta Constitution* (7/16/80).

2.1.60. "Four Murderers Flee From Reidsville," *Atlanta Constitution* (7/29/80).

2.1.61. "Three Escapees Caught in North Carolina; Body of Fourth Found in River," *Atlanta Journal* (7/30/80).

2.1.62. "Prison Escape Artist Blames Courts For Breakout," *Atlanta Journal & Constitution* (8/3/80).

2.1.63. "Reidsville Warden Still Optimistic," *Atlanta Constitution* (12/22/80).

2.1.64. "Reidsville Is Ripe For Violence," *Atlanta Constitution* (1/7/81).

2.1.65. "Monitor Says Reidsville Still Racist, Abusive," *Atlanta Journal* (1/7/81).

2.1.66. "Judge Alaimo Asked to Allow Full Integration at Reidsville," *Atlanta Constitution* (4/14/81).

2.1.67. "Reforming Reidsville: Court Monitor Strives to Join Hostile Forces," *Atlanta Journal & Constitution* (4/26/81).

2.1.68. "Reidsville Report: Work Areas Need Immediate Repairs," *Atlanta Journal* (6/19/81).

2.1.69. "State Contests Reidsville Monitor's Report," *Atlanta Journal* (7/9/81).

2.1.70. "Reidsville Prison Workers Get Collection of Reform Orders," *Columbus Enquirer* (7/16/81).

2.1.71. "Tight Prison Security Greets Visiting Judge," *Atlanta Journal* (7/22/81).

2.1.72. "Prison Has Problems, Monitor Says," *Augusta Chronicle* (7/30/81).

2.1.73. "Prison Officials Get Ultimatum," *Atlanta Constitution* (8/5/81).

2.1.74. "Reidsville 'Hell' Building Closed," *Atlanta Constitution* (3/9/82).

2.1.75. "Reidsville Prison Staff Ill-Equipped to Handle Problems, Expert Says," *Atlanta Journal* (3/9/82).

2.1.76. "Warden Planning to Leave Reidsville Prison," *Atlanta Journal* (4/12/82).

2.1.77. "Inmate Violence Kills Three at Reidsville," *Corrections Magazine* 8 (June 1982): 4.

2.1.78. "New Warden Returning Home," *Savannah Morning News* (6/20/82).

2.1.79. "Warden: Prison Reform Effort Failed," *Atlanta Journal* (6/28/82).

2.1.80. "Study Urges Options to Prison Terms," *Atlanta Journal* (9/13/82).

2.1.81. "On Guard and Angry at Reidsville," *Atlanta Journal & Constitution* (9/19/82).

2.1.82. "Saving Reidsville: Is it Worth the Cost," *Atlanta Journal & Constitution* (9/26/82).

2.1.83. "Warden at Reidsville Prison Is Disciplined," *Macon Telegraph & News* (11/24/82).

2.1.84. "State Says Court at Fault In Escapes," *Atlanta Journal* (12/13/82).

2.1.85. "Prisoners Escape In Fear," *Athens Banner-Herald* (12/14/82).

2.1.86. "Reidsville Conditions Dramatically Better, Court Monitor Finds," *Atlanta Constitution* (12/17/82).

2.1.87. "Study: Serious Security Flaws At Reidsville," *Atlanta Journal* (12/28/82).

2.1.88. "Bringing Georgia State Prison Into the 20th Century," *Atlanta Journal* (12/30/82).

2.1.89. "$75 an Hour: By the Hour, Prison Monitor Vincent Nathan is Georgia's Highest-paid Employee," *Augusta Chronicle* (1/26/83).

2.1.90. "Prison Style Democracy At Work: Reidsville Votes, 1000-Strong, For Disciplinary Plan," *Atlanta Journal & Constitution* (6/25/83).

2.1.91. "Reidsville Guards Say They Can't Fight Back," *Atlanta Constitution* (8/16/83).

2.1.92. "Harris Glad Reidsville Monitoring is Over," *Atlanta Constitution* (12/8/83).

2.1.93. "Prisons and Paroles: An Unsolved Equation," *Atlanta Journal & Constitution* (1/8/84).

2.1.94. "At Last: A Little Law & Order Behind Bars," *Macon Telegraph & News* (2/12/84).

2.1.95. "Full House in America's Prisons," *US News & World Report* (9/19/84).

2.1.96. "Inmate Recalls Stabbing In Suit Against Georgia," *Atlanta Constitution* (9/25/84).

2.1.97. "Inmate Loses Stabbing Suit," *Atlanta Constitution* (9/27/84).

2.1.98. "Guard: Warden Lied About Inmate Stabbing," *Atlanta Journal & Constitution* (10/16/84).

2.1.99. "Reidsville Now On the Road to Being a Model Prison," *Atlanta Journal & Constitution* (1/13/85).

2.1.100. "Escapee Had History of Mental Problems," *Atlanta Constitution* (6/21/85).

2.1.101. "After 13 Years, Reidsville Prison Reform Suit Ends," *Atlanta Constitution* (6/27/85).

2.1.102. "13-year Prison Suit Ends: $100 Million Worth of Changes Made," *Florida Times-Union* (6/27/85).

2.1.103. "Alaimo Ends Lawsuit Over State Prison," *Savannah Morning News* (6/27/85).

2.2. *Other Documents* include personal letters, agendas, meeting minutes, and internally used documents and reports. No meeting minutes were available for my use; all minutes of mediation, negotiation, and other meetings were marked "For Eyes Only" and had been taken out of the files loaned me by the Georgia attorney general's office. Similarly, internally used documents and reports were expunged from the case files kept by individual attorneys and parties to the case. Approximately 340 letters were included in the files. Most letters were written by defendants' counsel and plaintiffs' counsel, with others by Judge Alaimo, Special Master Pipkin, Special Monitor Nathan, and others. Two agendas were included in the files:

2.2.1. "The Georgia Prison System," prepared by the American Civil Liberties Union, Southern Regional Office, for presentation at the U.S. Civil Rights Commission hearings in Atlanta on November 16 and 17, 1973.

2.2.2. "Agenda: Court Ordered Prison Reform," meeting with Alabama state corrections and key law personnel to compare the *Guthrie* case with Alabama's *Pugh v. Locke*, on February 19, 1976.

Interviews. Key decision-makers in *Guthrie* were identified and contacted, and most were interviewed by the methods outlined in appendix A. Following are the names of all key decision-makers in *Guthrie* and (1) their position in the *Guthrie* case, (2) their location during the interview, (3) the date(s) of the interview, and (4) the manner of interview (in-person, telephone, or no interview) for each.

3.1. Anthony A. Alaimo; U.S. district judge; Reidsville, GA; June 26, 1985; in-person.

3.2. Allen Ault; DOR commissioner; Tallahassee, FL; February 28, 1986; in-person.

3.3. Samuel W. Austin; assistant DOR commissioner and GSP warden; Atlanta, GA; June 21, 1985; in-person.

3.4. David J. Bailey; Georgia assistant attorney general; Atlanta, GA; June 21, 1985; in-person.

3.5. Charles Balkcom; GSP warden; Reidsville, GA; June 26, 1985; in-person.

3.6. Dorothy T. Beasley; Georgia assistant attorney general; Atlanta, GA; July 16, 1985; in-person.

3.7. Charles Bell; independent monitor; Reidsville, GA; June 27, 1985; in-person.

3.8. Sanford Bishop; private counsel (plaintiffs); Columbus, GA; July 17, 1985; telephone.

3.9. Arthur K. Bolton; Georgia attorney general; Griffin, GA; November 7, 1985; telephone.

3.10. Michael J. Bowers; Georgia attorney general; Atlanta, GA; July 12, 1985; in-person.

3.11. E. B. "Jack" Caldwell; GSP warden; Reidsville, GA; July 18, 1985; telephone.

3.12. Richard Chambers; Georgia assistant attorney general; Decatur, GA; July 11, 1985; telephone.

3.13. Louise Clifton; GSP executive assistant; Reidsville, GA; June 27, 1985; in-person.

3.14. George H. Cox; assistant DOR commissioner; Statesboro, GA; November 14, 1985; telephone.

3.15. Robert Cullen; Georgia Legal Services; Atlanta, GA; July 16, 1985; in-person.

3.16. David C. Evans; DOR commissioner; Atlanta, GA; July 16, 1985; in-person.

3.17. Robert F. Greenwald; U.S. Department of Justice community relations service; no contact; no interview.

3.18. Marilyn Holifield; NAACP Legal Defense Fund; Tampa, FL; no interview.

3.19. Joseph S. Hopper; GSP warden; no contact; no interview.

3.20. William D. Kelley; Office of Planning and Budgeting planner; Atlanta, GA; July 11 and 16, 1985; in-person.

3.21. David L. G. King; Georgia assistant attorney general; Decatur, GA; July 11, 1985; in-person.

3.22. Harrison Kohler; Georgia assistant attorney general; Atlanta, GA; June 21, 1985; in-person.

3.23. John C. Jones; Georgia assistant attorney general; Atlanta, GA; June 21, 1985; in-person.

3.24. Don A. Langham; Georgia assistant attorney general; Atlanta, GA; July 10, 1985; telephone.

3.25. Ellis MacDougall; DOR commissioner; Columbia, SC; December 3, 1985; telephone.

3.26. Martha Miller; Georgia Legal Services; Atlanta, GA; July 16, 1985; in-person.

3.27. Charles M. Montgomery; GSP warden; Washington, DC; July 18, 1985; telephone.

3.28. Vincent M. Nathan; special monitor; Denver, CO; July 19, 1985; telephone.

3.29. Lanson Newsome; GSP warden; Reidsville, GA; June 27, 1985; in-person.

3.30. Marvin Pipkin; special master; Saint Simon's Island, GA; June 25, 1985; in-person.

3.31. Charles Steven Ralston; NAACP Legal Defense Fund; New York, NY; July 17, 1985; telephone.

3.32. Steve Rieck; Office of Planning and Budgeting planner; Atlanta, GA; July 11, 1985; in-person.

3.33. Daryl A. Robinson; Georgia assistant attorney general; Atlanta, GA; July 11, 1985; in-person.

3.34. Lucy C. Thompson; U.S. Department of Justice civil rights division; Washington, DC; July 8, 1985; telephone.

3.35. John C. Walden; Georgia assistant attorney general; Atlanta, GA; July 12, 1985; in-person.

3.36. Lynn Walker; NAACP Legal Defense Fund; New York, NY; no interview.

3.37. Steven L. Winter; NAACP Legal Defense Fund; New York, NY; July 17, 1985; telephone.

Direct Observations. The only direct observation in this case study of *Guthrie* involved observation of the final injunctive hearing at the GSP hearing room, Reidsville, Georgia, on June 26, 1985. This hearing is described in chapter 1.

Physical Artifacts. Physical evidence of the *Guthrie* case included tours of GSP facilities (June 26 and 27, 1985), visits to Judge Alaimo's courtroom in Brunswick, Georgia, on June 26, 1985, and visits to the offices of defendants, defendants' counsel, plaintiffs' counsel, and the negotiation suite at the Hilton Inn on Jekyll Island, Georgia.

Appendix C
Prison Reform Litigation in America

This appendix summarizes prison reform litigation state by state. It does not include the hundreds of lawsuits against municipal, county, and federal correctional institutions in the United States. A complete legal citation was not available for all cases summarized because court opinions have not been published in all cases (COOAGNAGF, 1980; Taggart, 1989; Feeley, 1989).

Alaska. A consent decree was approved in 1983 for the construction of Alaska's first high-security prison. Previously, Alaska sent all high-risk prisoners to federal prisons, mostly El Reno, OK; Marion, IL; Leavenworth, KS; and Lompoc, CA. These inmates sued in 1981 for violation of their visitation rights in that they were so far away from their families and friends.

Alabama. The entire state prison system is under court order (conditions and overcrowding), *Newman v. Alabama*, 466 F. Supp. 628 (M.D. Ala. 1979).

Arizona. The state penitentiary was challenged (conditions and overcrowding), *Harris v. Cardwell*, C.A. No. 75-185 PHX-CAM (D. Ariz.).

Arkansas. The entire state prison system is under court order (conditions and overcrowding), *Finney v. Hutto*, 410 F. Supp. 251 (E.D. Ark. 1976), *aff'd*, 548 F. 2d 740 (8th Cir. 1976), *aff'd*, 437 U.S. 678 (1978).

California. California's Department of Corrections director, Daniel McCarthy, has begun a program of prison construction using prefabricated concrete panels to build more than thirty thousand new prison beds after inmates' lawsuits were filed alleging overcrowded state prisons.

Colorado. The state maximum security penitentiary was challenged (conditions and overcrowding), *Ramos v. Lamm*, A.C. No. 77-K-1093 (D. Colo.).

Delaware. The state penitentiary is under court order (conditions and overcrowding), *Anderson v. Redman,* 429 F. Supp. 1105 (D. Del. 1977).

Florida. The entire state prison system was challenged (overcrowding), *Costello v. Wainwright,* 397 F. Supp. 20 (M.D. Fla. 1975), consent decree, 72-109-Civ.-J.S., entered October 1979.

Georgia. The state maximum security prison is under court order and consent decrees (conditions and overcrowding), *Guthrie v. Evans,* C.A. No. 73-3068 (S.D. Ga. 1986).

Illinois. The state prison at Menard was challenged (conditions and overcrowding), *Lightfoot v. Walker.*

Indiana. Prisons at Pendleton and Michigan City were challenged, *French v. Owens and Wellman v. Faulkner,* IP-37-C (S.D. Ind.).

Louisiana. The state penitentiary is under court order (conditions and overcrowding), *Williams v. Edward,* 547 F. 2d 1026 (5th Cir. 1977).

Maryland. The two state prisons are under court order (overcrowding), *Johnson v. Levine,* 450 F. Supp. 648 (D. Md. 1978), *aff'd in part, rev'd in part,* 588 F. 2d 1378 (4th Cir. 1978); *Nelson v. Collins,* 455 F. Supp. 727 (D. Md. 1978), *rev'd in part, aff'd in part,* 588 F. 2d 1378 (4th Cir. 1978).

Massachusetts. The maximum security unit at the state prison in Walpole was challenged (conditions), *Blake v. Hall,* C.A. 78-3051-T (D. Mass).

Mississippi. The entire state prison system is under court order (conditions and overcrowding), *Gates v. Collier,* 349 F. Supp. 881 (N.D. Miss. 1972), 380 F. Supp. 482 (N.D. Miss. 1975), *aff'd,* 525 F. 2d 965 (5th Cir. 1976).

Missouri. The maximum security prison is under court order (conditions and overcrowding), *Burks v. Graham,* 75 cv.149-c (E.D. Mo.).

Nevada. The two major prisons have been challenged (conditions and overcrowding), *Maginnis v. O'Callaghan,* C.A. No. 77-0221 (D. Nev.).

New Hampshire. The state penitentiary is under court order (conditions and overcrowding), *Laaman v. Helgemoe,* 437 F. Supp. 269 (D. N.H. 1977).

New Mexico. The state penitentiary was challenged (conditions and overcrowding), *Duran v. Apodaca,* A.C. No. 77-721-C (D. N.M.).

North Carolina. The entire state prison system was challenged (conditions and overcrowding), *Bolding v. Holshouser*, 575 F. 2d 461 (4th Cir. 1978), *cert. denied*, 99 S. Ct. 121 (1978).

Ohio. The state prisons at Lucasville and Columbus are under court order (conditions and overcrowding), *Chapman v. Rhodes*, 434 F. Supp. 1007 (S.D. Ohio 1977); *Stewart v. Rhodes*, Order No. C-2-78-220 (E.D. Ohio 12/4/78).

Oklahoma. The state penitentiary is under court order (conditions), while the entire state prison system is under orders (overcrowding), *Battle v. Anderson*, 477 F. Supp. 516 (E.D. Okla. 1977).

Rhode Island. The entire state prison system is under court order (conditions and overcrowding), *Palmigiano v. Garrahy*, 443 F. Supp. 956 (D. R.I. 1977).

South Carolina. The state prison was challenged (conditions and overcrowding), *Mattison v. South Carolina Board of Corrections*, C.A. No. 76-318 (D. S.C.).

Tennessee. The entire state prison system is under court order (conditions), *Trigg v. Blanton*, C.A. No. A6047 (Davidson Co., Tenn. Ch. App. August 23, 1978).

Texas. The entire state prison system is under court order (conditions and overcrowding), *Ruiz v. Estelle*, Civ. No. 5523 (E.D. Tex.).

Utah. The state prison was challenged (conditions and overcrowding), *Neilson v. Matheson*.

Virginia. The state department of corrections has built two prefabricated prisons to relieve overcrowding after inmates launched lawsuits over conditions and overcrowding.

Vermont. The state prison was closed after inmates launched a prison reform lawsuit challenging conditions and practices.

Washington. The state reformatory was challenged (conditions and overcrowding), *Collins v. Rhay*, C.A. No. C78-13-V (W.D. Wash.).

Wyoming. The state prison is operating under stipulations and consent decrees, *Bustos v. Herschler*, C.A. No. C76-143-B (D. Wyo.).

District of Columbia. The DC jails are under court order (conditions and overcrowding), *Campbell v. McGruder*, 416 F. Supp. 100, *aff'd in part*, 580 F. 2d 521 (D.C. Cir. 1978).

Appendix D

Contrast between Conventional Adjudication and Institutional Reform Litigation

Elements	Conventional Adjudication	Institutional Reform
The Issue	Likely to be of private rights and duties. If public body involved, issue likely to be procedural	Likely to involve substantive rights and means of compelling a public body to effectuate those rights
Parties	Likely to be one "person" suing another	Likely to be a class of individuals suing a class of officials, public institutions, and political entities
Critical facts	Historical (what has happened) and adjudicative (relevant to rights and liabilities of the two parties)	Predictive (situation as it is likely to exist during life of decree) and legislative (relevant to continuing decree)
Governing Principle	Legal precedents	Strategy, tactics, and potential outcomes not informed by legal precedent
Taking of Evidence	Adversary hearing and rules of evidence	Wide participation, relaxed standards, more expert witnesses
Relief Sought	Declaration, negative injunction, damages; normally narrow, closely tied to legal injury	Affirmative injunction, affecting many beyond parties; potentially broad
Framing of Decree	Imposed by court after hearing evidence	Large amount of negotiation
Impact	Confined to parties	Affects large segment of society
Duration of Court Involvement	One-time judgment	Continuing decree; subject to reopening and amendment
Role of Judge	Passive; adjudicative in resolving dispute between two parties in a one-time, normally self-executing judgment	Active; legislative in framing criteria; executive in implementing decree
Review	Abuse of discretion and error of law; sufficiency of evidence and legal precedents important	Contribution of appellate court to policy, strategy, and tactics more important than monitoring fact findings or legal principles

Source: Coffin, 1979, p. 989.

Appendix E

Groups in *Guthrie v. Evans*

This list is based on a study of archives, documents, and interviews, where some individuals were far more extensively involved in the lawsuit than others. The list was checked against the advice of others, including interviewees. (* = key decision-makers in *Guthrie*)

Plaintiffs' Counsel	The Court	Defendants' Counsel
Original Counsel	*1972 Judge*	*Attorneys General*
Sanford Bishop*	Albert Henderson	Arthur Bolton*
Law Partners	*1973–86 Judge*	Michael Bowers*
Ralph Hudlin	Anthony A. Alaimo*	*Assistant Attorneys*
Herbert Phipps		*General*
LDF Attorneys	*Court-Appointed*	Dorothy Beasley*
Lynn Walker*	*Personnel*	Don A. Langham*
Marilyn Holifield*	*Mediator*	David J. Bailey*
Jack Greenberg	Robert F. Greenwald,	James L. Mackay
Henrietta Turnquest	US Department of	David L. G. King*
Stanley A. Bass	Justice*	John C. Walden*
C. Steven Ralston*	*Amicus Curiae*	Richard Chambers*
Steven L. Winter*	Lucy C. Thompson, US	Nicholas Dumich
GA Legal Services	Department of Justice*	G. Thomas Davis
Robert Cullen*	*Special Masters*	John Dunsmore
Martha Miller*	Jack S. Hutto	Harold Hill
NAACP	Eugene Tillman	Carl C. Jones
George Hairston	John H. Thomas	H. Andrew Owen
	Marvin L. Pipkin*	Robert Stubbs
Plaintiffs	*Special Monitor*	Courtney Stanton
Original Plaintiffs	Vincent M. Nathan*	Harrison Kohler*
Arthur S. Guthrie	*Assistants to*	Michael S. Bailey
Joseph Coggins II	*Special Monitor*	Marion Gordon
[50 inmates who	Daniel Cron	Daryl Robinson*
signed the 1972	Frederick Byers	John C. Jones*
complaint]	Judith Heck	
	Independent Monitor	
	Charles Bell*	

Plaintiffs (con't.)	*The Court* (con't.)	*Defendants*
1973–83 Class	*Court-Appointed*	*DOR Commissioners*
Action Members	*Experts*	Ellis MacDougall*
[all black inmates at	Samuel W. Hoover	Allen Ault*
GSP, except those	Rodney Hoover	David C. Evans*
who expressly	Harry Markel	*DOR Assistant*
waived their right	John Hulla	*Commissioners*
to sue]	Lambert N. King	Samuel W. Austin*
	Jay Harness	George H. Cox
1983–86 Class Action	James D. Henderson	*Governors' OPB*
Members	Seth Hirshorn	*Planners*
[all inmates at GSP,		Steven Rieck*
white and black,		William D. Kelley*
since the class action		*GSP Wardens*
was certified in		E. B. "Jack" Caldwell*
1973]		Joseph S. Hopper*
		Charles Balkcom*
		Samuel W. Austin*
		Charles M. Montgomery*
		Lanson Newsome*
		GSP Executive
		Assistant
		Louise Clifton*

Appendix F

Costs in *Guthrie v. Evans*, FY1976–FY1986

Fiscal Year	Staff #	Personnel	Operations	Medical	*Subtotal*	Cannery
1976	455	4,710,681	3,251,746	194,689	8,157,116	
1977	504	5,083,974	2,803,842	639,640	8,527,456	
1978	524	5,911,645	3,793,872	1,274,719	10,980,236	
1979	604	7,357,205	3,473,819	1,234,290	12,065,305	
1980	619	8,119,770	3,634,336	1,519,380	13,273,486	1,432,182
1981	624	9,058,240	4,435,738	2,447,325	15,941,303	1,859,810
1982	705	10,819,403	2,919,053	2,174,000	15,912,456	2,154,839
1983	953	12,810,655	4,400,651	2,511,435	19,722,741	2,066,132
1984	953	15,317,835	4,084,814	2,069,434	21,472,083	2,387,430
1985	1058	17,430,365	4,289,055	2,172,906	23,892,326	2,400,000
1986	1151	19,435,613	4,503,508	2,281,551	26,220,672	2,500,000

Source: DOR, 1982. Please note that the figures for FY1984–FY1986 were estimates made in 1982 by the DOR.

Capital	Legal	*Total*	*Explanation*
375,000	85,475	8,617,591	Capital: feed mill & irrigation
1,082,000	92,000	9,701,456	New positions: 48 C.O.s; Capital: cannery, meat plant & irrigation
583,925	137,990	11,702,151	New positions: 16 C.O.s, 2 counselors, 2 food serve; Capital: cannery, kitchen, baths & sewage
8,661,852	125,000	20,852,157	New positions: 72 C.O.s, 6 health, 2 counselors; Capital: Project 360, Unit B, Project 90, Units L & M, cannery & barns
6,932,813	875,816	22,514,297	New positions: 8 health, 1 sales, 1 technical instructor, 1 cannery; Capital: Project 360, renovation & sewage
21,881,390	191,780	39,874,283	New positions: 4 food, 1 librarian; Capital: Project 360—A, B & C; fire safety
	258,000	18,325,295	New positions: 81 C.O.s for Guthrie compliance
8,555,100	300,000	30,643,973	New positions: 224 C.O.s; 24 misc.; Capital: Maxi-Max security Unit, fire safety, Unit C
10,426,970	300,000	34,586,483	Capital: Units D, L & M
	200,000	26,492,326	New positions: 105 C.O.s
	100,000	28,820,672	New positions: 93 C.O.s and closing of Unit H

Notes

Chapter 2

1. Observations recorded in the chronology of *Guthrie* in chapters 2 through 5 refer generally to data described in appendix A, including archival records, other documents, direct observations, physical artifacts, and interviews with key decision-makers in the case. Because anonymity was promised to the key decision-makers upon whose comments much of this chronology was based, there are no specific interview references.

2. Burns negotiated for a pardon with Governor Arnall in 1943, but the Georgia State Pardon and Parole Board refused to free him as long as Burns remained a fugitive. In 1945, Burns returned to Georgia with his second wife, Clara, telling her, "[I]n all people's lives there comes a time when one must show courage." With Arnall as his counsel, Burns faced the board. They erased the prison sentence and restored his full civil rights. Burns died in a veterans hospital in 1955 at the age of 65.

3. Robert P. Balkcom was warden at GSP for nearly seventeen years (January 1, 1948, to December 10, 1965), the longest time served in that position by any warden. It is interesting to note that he refused to witness any of the approximately 150 executions at GSP. Although it was tradition for the warden to witness the execution of inmates, Balkcom didn't believe in the death penalty and became physically ill at the thought of it.

Chapter 3

1. Due to obvious security risks involved, architectural renderings and blueprints of the renovated GSP and Rogers Correctional Institution were not available.

Chapter 5

1. Plaintiffs also submitted their findings of fact (ordered due by July 30, 1978) to Special Master Pipkin in May 1979.

2. On Tuesday, August 7, 1979, about one hundred citizens left Savannah for Reidsville to protest prison conditions there. The Rev. Hosea Williams, then Georgia state representative (D-Atlanta) and former field organizer for

Martin Luther King, Jr., led the group from Savannah's Forsyth Park. He described GSP to the press as "Georgia's combination of a Nazi Concentration Camp and an old slave labor plantation" (*Atlanta Constitution*, 8/7/79, p. 1A). A state court ordered that the marchers come no closer to GSP than a nearby highway bridge. Unfortunately, one nineteen-year-old protester, Arthur Norwood, drowned while attempting to swim across the river (*Atlanta Journal*, 8/9/79). Seven other civil rights workers were taken into custody for crossing the bridge but vowed to continue a hunger strike while in jail (*Atlanta Journal*, 8/13/79).

3. At this time in the *Guthrie* proceedings (November 20, 1979), the important non-procedural remedial decrees included the November 26, 1976, protective order, comprehensive consent decrees of July 19, August 4, and December 1, 1978, and the judge's re-integration order of December 12, 1978.

4. Special Monitor Nathan later gave a gruesome depiction of the 1979 conditions and practice at GSP. "[Nathan's] report on Reidsville took him seven months to finish and ran to 450 pages. In it he documented dungeonlike conditions as well as what he called 'a reign of terror' against inmates. . . . The year before, wrote Nathan, a riot at Reidsville had left one guard and two inmates dead. Afterward, inmates were subjected to sustained, rampant brutality on a daily basis. They were routinely beaten, maced, and shot with 'stun guns' loaded with canvas-covered lead pellets. Guards walked the cell blocks wielding illegal knives and pickax handles. Unruly prisoners were strip-searched and thrown into segregation cells empty of everything except a filthy, urine-soaked mattress. Mentally ill or retarded inmates lived with the rest of the prison population, where they were abused by other prisoners and maced by guards when they made too much noise. Some disturbed prisoners were in the habit of smearing excrement over themselves, and lived covered in their own feces and surrounded by filth. . . . Parts of the prison were racially segregated, and Nathan found widespread discrimination on the part of the mostly white staff. Weevils, cockroaches, and rat droppings were found in prison kitchens. Sanitation experts hired by Nathan found a high frequency of food poisoning and conditions ripe for an epidemic of tuberculosis" (Pollock, 1983, p. 97).

5. Nathan was surprised when Warden Balkcom was fired by the DOR, commenting later, "I didn't request or expect it" (Pollock, 1983, p. 7).

6. Austin spent nearly all his time from late April through June 1980 preparing GSP for the first prospective execution in Georgia since 1964. A fellow DOR assistant commissioner, George Cox, resigned from the DOR to protest the impending execution. A last-minute appeal on June 5, 1980, successfully averted execution of the sentence that was scheduled for June 6, 1980. Austin also developed new inmate grievance procedures dealing with

inmate allegations of physical and verbal abuse by staff. Steps were also taken toward achieving compliance and establishing task forces to plan for the major changes to come.

7. Nathan has been a special master in the Texas case since 1981.

8. In 1987, GSP was fully accredited by the National Corrections Association (NCA).

Bibliography

Ault, Allen L. 1980. Resource Utilization in Corrections. *Corrections Today* 42: 12.

Ball, Howard, Dale Krane, and Thomas P. Lauth. 1982. *Compromised Compliance: Implementation of the 1965 Voting Rights Act.* Westport, CT: Greenwood Press.

Baum, Lawrence. 1977. Judicial Impact as a Form of Policy Implementation. In John A. Gardiner, ed., *Public Law and Public Policy.* New York: Praeger Publishers.

Boston, John. 1981. Consent Decrees: Approval, Enforceability and Modification. In Alvin J. Bronstein, ed., *Representing Prisoners.* Washington, DC: Practicing Law Institute.

Bradley, Valerie I., and Gary J. Clarke, eds. 1976. *Paper Victories and Hard Realities: The Implementation of the Legal and Constitutional Rights of the Mentally Disabled.* Washington, DC: The Health Policy Center.

Brakel, Samuel Jan. 1986. Mastering the Legal Access Rights of Prison Inmates. *New England Journal on Criminal and Civil Confinement* 12: 1–69.

———. 1986. Prison Reform Litigation: Has the Revolution Gone Too Far? *Judicature* 70: 5–6, 64–65.

Bronstein, Alvin J., ed. 1981. *Representing Prisoners.* Washington, DC: Practicing Law Institute.

Burns, Robert Elliot. 1931. *I Am a Fugitive from a Georgia Chain Gang.* Detroit, MI: Gale Research Co. (1972 reprint).

Cavanagh, Ralph, and Austin Sarat. 1980. Thinking about Courts: Toward and Beyond a Jurisprudence of Judicial Competence. *Law & Society Review* 14: 371–420.

Chayes, Abram. 1976. The Role of the Judge in Public Law Litigation. *Harvard Law Review* 89: 1281–1316.

Clear, Todd R., and George F. Cole. 1986. *American Corrections.* Monterey, CA: Brooks/Cole Publishing Co.

Coffin, Frank M. 1979. The Frontier of Remedies: A Call for Exploration. *California Law Review* 67: 983–99.

Comment. 1970. Enforcement of Judicial Financing Orders: Constitutional Rights in Search of a Remedy. *Georgetown Law Journal* 59: 393.

Comment. 1976. Equitable Remedies: An Analysis of Judicial Utilization of Neoreceivership to Implement Large Scale Institutional Change. *Wisconsin Law Review* 1976: 1161–1200.

COOAGNAAGF (Committee on the Office of Attorney General of the National Association of Attorneys General Foundation). 1980. *Implementation of Remedies in Prison Conditions Suits.* Raleigh, NC: National Association of Attorneys General Foundation.

Cooke, James, and Thomas Panko. 1986. The *Gates v. Collier* Case. Presented at the annual meeting of the Southern Conference on Corrections, Tallahassee, Florida.

Cooper, Phillip J. 1985. Conflict or Constructive Tension: The Changing Relationship of Judges and Administrators. *Public Administration Review* 45: 643.

————. 1988. *Hard Judicial Choices: Federal District Court Judges and State and Local Officials.* New York: Oxford University Press.

Crouch, Ben M., and James W. Marquart. 1985. Judicial Reform and Prisoner Control: The Impact of *Ruiz v. Estelle* on a Texas Penitentiary. *Law & Society Review* 19: 557–86.

————. 1990. *An Appeal to Justice: Litigation Reform of Texas Prisons.* Austin: University of Texas Press.

Department of Offender Rehabilitation. 1982. Corrections Briefing Document: *Guthrie v. Evans* Lawsuit at Georgia State Prison. Atlanta, GA: Georgia Department of Corrections.

DiIulio, John J., Jr. 1987. *Governing Prisons: A Comparative Study of Correctional Management.* New York: Free Press.

————, ed. 1990. *Courts, Corrections, and the Constitution: The Impact of Judicial Intervention on Prisons and Jails.* New York: Oxford University Press.

Diver, Colin S. 1979. The Judge as Political Powerbroker: Superintending Structural Change in Public Institutions. *Virginia Law Review* 65: 43–106.

Drake, Jack. 1981. Judicial Implementation and *Wyatt v. Stickney. Alabama Law Review* 32: 299–312.

Dworkin, Ronald. 1978. *Taking Rights Seriously.* Cambridge, MA: Harvard University Press.

————. 1985. *A Matter of Principle.* Cambridge, MA: Harvard University Press.

Eisenberg, Theodore, and Stephen C. Yeazell. 1980. The Ordinary and the Extraordinary in Institutional Litigation. *Harvard Law Review* 93: 465–517.

Ekland-Olson, Sheldon. 1986. Crowding, Social Control, and Prison Violence: Evidence from the Post-Ruiz Years in Texas. *Law & Society Review* 20: 389–421.

Engel, Kathleen, and Stanley Rothman. 1984. The Paradox of Prison Reform: Rehabilitation, Prisoners' Rights and Violence. *Harvard Journal of Law and Public Policy* 7: 413–42.

Feeley, Malcolm M. 1989. The Significance of Prison Conditions Cases: Budgets and Regions. *Law & Society Review* 23: 273–82.

Fiss, Owen M. 1978. *The Civil Rights Injunction.* Bloomington, IN: Indiana University Press.

———. 1979. Foreword: The Forms of Justice. *Harvard Law Review* 93: 1–58.

———. 1984. Against Settlement. *Yale Law Journal* 93: 1073.

Flathman, Richard E. 1976. *The Practice of Rights.* Cambridge, England: Cambridge University Press.

Fox, Vernon. 1985. *Introduction to Corrections,* 3rd ed. Englewood Cliffs, NJ: Prentice Hall.

Fuller, Lon L. 1978. The Forms and Limits of Adjudication. *Harvard Law Review* 92: 353–409.

Glazer, Nathan. 1978. Should Courts Administer Social Services? *Public Interest* 50: 64–80.

Hale, George E. 1979. Federal Courts and the State Budgetary Process. *Administration & Society* 11: 357–68.

Hanson, Roger A. 1986. *The Resolution of State Prisoner Grievances in the Federal Courts.* Washington, DC: National Institute of Justice.

Harriman, Linda, and Jeffrey D. Straussman. 1983. Do Judges Determine Budget Decisions? Federal Court Decisions in Prison Reform and State Spending for Corrections. *Public Administration Review* 43: 343–51.

Harris, M. Kay, and Dudley P. Spiller, Jr. 1976. *After Decision: Implementation of Judicial Decrees in Correctional Settings.* Washington, DC: U.S. Government Printing Office.

Hawkes, Mary Ann. 1985. Rhode Island: A Case Study in Compliance. *Corrections Today* 47: 167–73, 183.

Horowitz, Donald L. 1977. *The Courts and Social Policy.* Washington, DC: The Brookings Institution.

Jacobs, James B. 1977. *Stateville: The Penitentiary in Mass Society.* Chicago: University of Chicago Press.

———. 1981. The Prisoners' Rights Movement and Its Impacts, 1960–1980. In Norval Morris and Michael Tonry, eds., *Crime and Justice: An Annual Review of Research.* Chicago: University of Chicago Press.

Johnson, Frank M. 1982. The Role of the Federal Courts in Institutional Litigation. *Alabama Law Review* 32: 271–79.

Justice, William Wayne. 1984. Protecting Inmates' Constitutional Rights: A Shared Responsibility. *Corrections Today* 46: 58–62.

Kennedy, Robert F., Jr. 1978. *Judge Frank M. Johnson, Jr.: A Biography.* New York: G. P. Putnam's Sons.

Leeke, William D. 1980. The Negotiated Settlement: Prisoners' Rights in Action. In Geoffrey P. Alpert, ed., *Legal Rights of Prisoners.* Beverly Hills, CA: Sage Publications.

Levine, David I. 1984. The Authority for the Appointment of Remedial Special Masters in Federal Institutional Reform Litigation: The History Reconsidered. *U.C. Davis Law Review* 17: 753.

Levinson, Marc R. 1982. Special Masters: Engineers of Court-Ordered Reform. *Corrections Magazine* 8: 6–18.

Liles, Richard Joe. 1987. An Analysis of the Use of Special Masters for Assuring Compliance with Judicial Decrees in Corrections Litigation. D.P.A. diss., Western Michigan University.

Low, Peter W., and John Calvin Jeffries, Jr. 1988. *Civil Rights Actions: Section 1983 and Related Statutes.* Westbury, NY: Foundation Press.

Lumumba, N. 1979. Letter to the Editor. *GSP News* (January).

McDowell, Gary L. 1984. A Scrupulous Regard for the Rightful Independence of the States: Justice Stone and the Limits of Federal Equity Power. *Harvard Journal of Law and Public Policy* 7: 507–19.

Martin, Steven J., and Sheldon Eklund-Olson. 1987. *Texas Prisons: The Walls Come Tumbling Down.* Austin: Texas Monthly Press.

Melnick, R. Shep. 1985. The Politics of Partnership. *Public Administration Review* 45: 653–60.

Moss, Kathryn. 1985. The Catalytic Effect of a Federal Court Decision on a State Legislature. *Law & Society Review* 19: 147–57.

Munro, Jim L. 1986. The Impact of Litigation on Managerial Reform: The Corrections Case. Presented at the annual meeting of the Southern Conference on Corrections, Tallahassee, Florida.

Nagel, Robert F. 1984. Controlling the Structural Injunction. *Harvard Journal of Law and Public Policy* 7: 395–411.

Nathan, Vincent. 1979. The Use of Masters in Institutional Reform Litigation. *University of Toledo Law Review* 10: 419–64.

Palmer, John W. 1985. *Constitutional Rights of Prisoners,* 3rd ed. Cincinnati, OH: Anderson Publishing Co.

Pollock, Ellen Joan. 1983. Q: What's a Toledo Lawyer Doing in a Georgia Prison? A: Running It. *The American Lawyer* 5: 97–99.

Rawls, John. 1971. *A Theory of Justice.* Cambridge, MA: Belknap Press.

Rich, Thomas F., and Arnold I. Barnett. 1985. Model-Based U.S. Prison Population Projections. *Public Administration Review* 45: 780–89.

Richards, David A. J. 1977. Rules, Policies, and Neutral Principles: The Search for Legitimacy in Common Law and Constitutional Adjudication. *Georgia Law Review* 11: 1069–1114.

Rivers, E. D. 1938. Prison Reform in Georgia. *The Atlantian* 1: 4–5, 21.

Rosenbloom, David H. 1983. *Public Administration and Law: Bench v. Bureau in the United States.* New York: Marcel Dekker.

———. 1988. Public Administration and the Judiciary: The "New Partnership." *Public Administration Review* 47: 75.

Rothman, David J., and Sheila M. Rothman. 1984. *The Willowbrook Wars.* New York: Harper & Row.

Rowat, Donald C. 1986. *The Ombudsman Plan: The Worldwide Spread of an Idea.* Lanham, MD: University Press of America.

Scheingold, Stuart A. 1974. *The Politics of Rights: Lawyers, Public Policy, and Political Change.* New Haven, CT: Yale University Press.

Sherman, Michael, and Gordon Hawkins. 1981. *Imprisonment in America: Choosing the Future.* Chicago: University of Chicago Press.

Southern Conference on Corrections. 1986. Roundtable: Responses to Conditions Suits: Renovation or New Construction. Presented at the annual meeting of the Southern Conference on Corrections, Tallahassee, Florida.

Straussman, Jeffrey D. 1986. Courts and Public Purse Strings: Have Portraits of Budgeting Missed Something? *Public Administration Review* 46: 345–51.

Sturm, Susan. 1990. Resolving the Remedial Dilemma: Strategies of Judicial Intervention in Prisons. *University of Pennsylvania Law Review* 138: 805–912.

Sykes, Gresham. 1958. *The Society of Captives.* Princeton, NJ: Princeton University Press.

Taggart, William A. 1986. The Impact of Court-Ordered Prison Reform on State Expenditures for Corrections. Presented at the annual meeting of the Academy of Criminal Justice Science, Orlando, Florida.

———. 1989. Redefining the Power of the Federal Judiciary: The Impact of Court-Ordered Prison Reform on State Expenditures for Corrections. *Law & Society Review* 23: 241–71.

Trubeck, David M., Joel B. Grossman, William L. F. Felstiner, Herbert M. Kritzer, Austin Sarat. 1987. *Civil Litigation Research Project Final Report,* 3rd ed. Madison, WI: Disputes Processing Research Program.

Weinstein, Jack B. 1982. The Effect of Austerity on Institutional Litigation. *Law and Human Behavior* 6: 145–51.

Williams, Patricia J. 1987. Alchemical Notes: Reconstructing Ideals from Deconstructed Rights. *Harvard Civil Rights—Civil Liberties Law Review* 22: 401–33.

Yackle, Larry W. 1989. *Reform and Regret: The Story of Federal Judicial Involvement in the Alabama Prison System.* New York: Oxford University Press.

Yarbrough, Tinsley E. 1981. *Judge Frank M. Johnson and Human Rights in Alabama.* Tuscaloosa: University of Alabama Press.

———. 1982. The Judge as Manager: The Case of Judge Frank Johnson. *Journal of Policy Analysis & Management* 1: 386–400.

———. 1984. The Alabama Prison Litigation. *Justice System Journal* 9: 276.

———. 1985. The Political World of Federal Judges as Managers. *Public Administration Review* 45: 660–66.

Yin, Robert K. 1984. *Case Study Research: Design and Methods.* Beverly Hills, CA: Sage Publications.

Index

Activists, judges seen as, 96–97

Adjudication, 5–6, 10–12, 133. *See also* Judges/Judiciary

Administrative segregation, at GSP, 13, 37, 38, 41, 48, 66; consent decrees on, 46, 49; improvement of cells in, 60, 61

Afro-American culture and history, library holdings in, 51, 97

Alabama prison reform litigation, 14–15, 24, 45, 95, 105, 130; compared with *Guthrie*, 34; impact studies of, 9, 11–12; prison placed in receivership, 54, 55; remedial decrees, 106

Alabama prisons, 102, 103, 104

Alaimo, Judge Anthony A., 1–2, 23–24, 41–42, 47, 91–93, 107; adjudication of rights, 57, 58, 67, 101; appointment of Special Master, 32–33; assessments of, 79–80, 97; granting *Guthrie* class action status, 13, 25–26; as key decision-maker, 74, 75–76, 78; in liability phase, 31, 36; orders on segregation and desegregation, 30–31, 39; in post-decree phase, 56–58, 59, 60, 61, 65–66, 67, 69–71; in remedy phase, 45, 49, 51, 52, 95–96; role in mediation, 28–29, 30, 31–32

Alaska prison reform litigation, 130

Alcatraz of the Piney Woods, as nickname for GSP, 16

Amicus curiae. See Civil Rights Division, DOJ

Appeals courts, U.S., 6, 48, 54

Appeals process, 44, 106; not used in *Guthrie*, 45, 95, 106

Arizona prison reform litigation, 130

Arkansas prison reform litigation, 14, 24, 74, 102, 107, 130; responses to, 104, 105

Arkansas prisons, 103

Arnall (Ga. gov.), 139n 2

Arson, suspected in GSP chapel fire, 38

Assertiveness of inmates, as pressure in prison reform litigation, 102, 103–4

Association, right to, 28

Atlanta Journal, on 1972 *in forma pauperis*, 21–22

Attorneys, 27, 49, 91, 92, 106; as key decision-makers, 74–76, 77–78, 82. *See also* Legal assistance; NAACP Legal Defense Fund; *attorneys by name*

Attorneys general, 77, 78. *See also attorneys general by name*

Augusta (Ga.) Medical and Correctional Facility, 42, 61

Ault, Allen L., 30–31, 35

Austin, Samuel W. (GSP warden), 46, 62, 65, 70, 105, 140n 6

Bailey, David J., 30, 32, 33–34, 46, 75

Balkcom, Charles (GSP warden), 50–51, 59, 60, 61–62, 140n 5

Balkcom, Robert P. (GSP warden), 17, 50, 139n 3

Barnett, Arnold I., 102

Battle v. Anderson, 55, 132

Beasley, Dorothy T., 22, 23, 24, 25, 28, 30, 75

Beasley, Joseph, 30

Bell, Charles, 71

Bell, Griffin, Jr., 35

Bell v. Wolfish, 6

Beto, George, 105

Bishop, Sanford D., Jr., 22–23, 25–26, 27, 28, 32, 34

Black Muslim inmates. *See* Muslim inmates

Blacks, 13, 20, 26, 104; hiring of as correctional officers, 18, 29, 36–37

Bolton, Arthur K. (Ga. att. gen.), 18, 22, 30, 37, 47, 75

Books, inmate. *See* Literature, inmate

Bounds v. Smith, 48